This book is dedicated to the blood of my blood, the future generations of Cowarts who will one day read, hear, and carry forward this story. It is a living legacy, written in my own words, so my descendants will never have to rely on someone else's version of who their grandfather or great-grandfather was.

ACKNOWLEDGEMENTS

I want to take a moment to thank the people who played a major part in my journey not just in building my business, but in shaping the man behind it.

To **God,** I couldn't do any of this without YOU and I am forever grateful.

To **Estie Chanowitz**, you were the first person who gave me a shot. You introduced me to the Jewish community and believed in me before the world did. You gave me my first contract, my first chance, and opened the door that changed everything. My reputation and success began with the opportunity you entrusted to me.

To **Michal Zagury**, you helped me reach the next level. You believed in my potential when my company was still finding its footing. You could have walked away, but instead, you gave me the grace and space to grow. That patience allowed me to refine my business and elevate my brand.

To **Zalman Shepiro,** you were the one I had a thousand questions for. I received a lot of business advice and momentum from our conversations and you pointing me in the right place.

Each of you represents a cornerstone of my growth, and for that, I'm forever grateful.

This book and the man I've become wouldn't exist without your belief in me.

TABLE OF CONTENTS

Chapter 1: Secret Double Life	1
Chapter 2: Don't Run From Discipline	4
Chapter 3: Dreaming Beyond What You See	11
Chapter 4: Moments of Truth from my real-life experiences	19
chapter 6: Identity Crisis	43
chapter 7: Question We All Love	45
Chapter 8: Roller Coaster: Execution is Essential	47
chapter 9: Importance Of Having Good Credit	51
chapter 10: Lead By Example	55
Chapter 11: Relationships vs business	59
Chapter 12: Fighting Complacency and Building Discipline	63
Chapter 13: Finding My Path	67
Chapter 14: The Only Way Out, Was Straight Through	75
Chapter 15: A Man Does What He Needs to Do, No Matter What	79
Chapter 16: The Land of Dreamers	83
Chapter 17: In life, believe nothing you hear and half of what you see.	87
Chapter 18: Pizza as a Universal Analogy	89
Chapter 19: The Meaning of Life Is to Live	91
Chapter 20: Eviction	93

Chapter 21: Sometimes you learn it the "hard way" 97
Chapter 22: No Pain, No Gain 99
Chapter 23: Life Irony 101
Chapter 24: Everyone Has a Role 103
Chapter 25: It's Okay Not to Fit In 105
chapter 26: "Alignment Over Ego" 107
Chapter 27: Somethings you might not know about me 109
Chapter 28: Dr frankenstein 113
Closing Words 115
About the Author 119

CHAPTER 1
Secret Double Life

"Oh my God... he doesn't have a diploma."

That's what I always imagined people would say if they found out. And for years, I carried that weight like a brick in my back pocket.

In 2010, I should've been walking across that stage, grabbing my paper, and tossing my cap in the air. But I didn't. Not because I was lazy. or couldn't keep up in class. I had all my credits. I failed the FCAT reading by four points. Four. The passing score was 300. I got a 296.

Back then, Florida made you pass that thing to graduate. They stopped the very next year, which still feels like one of life's sick jokes. I even missed one of the retakes because I got into a stupid accident and fell off the hood of a moving car at about 35 miles an hour. Rolled across the asphalt like a burnt sausage. Two weeks later, still itching and peeling, I'm sitting in a freezing classroom taking the makeup test... the only student in the room.

I didn't pass.

That failure turned into an anxiety that followed me for years. At night, I couldn't sleep. Every movie or TV show with a graduation scene felt like it was mocking me. I started falling asleep with the

TV on just to quiet my thoughts and it had to be feel-good comedies: Fresh Prince, My Wife and Kids, King of Queens. No drama. Just laughter and family vibes.

Years later, living back at my parents' house after getting evicted, I saw a sign: Fort Lauderdale Adult, Get Your Diploma. I walked in and signed up. I thought I had to take weeks of classes before testing, so I went once a week, half-asleep from my overnight shift.

By this time, I was dating my now-wife. She had an associate's and a bachelor's in criminal justice. I never told her I didn't have my diploma. That meant every week I was lying about where I was going, making up excuses so she wouldn't just pop up at my parents' house or the park. I was hiding like I was having an affair... with a GED program.

Three months in, someone says, "You know you could've taken the test on day one, right?" I'd been wasting gas, wasting time, and lying for nothing?...mannnnnnnn.

I scheduled the test immediately. It had three parts: math, reading, and science.

Math – I've always been solid at it. Passed with a high score.

Reading – This time, I read every single page. No shortcuts. Passed.

Science – Formulas, logic, numbers. Passed.

I got home, checked my score online, and saw the words: Congratulations on your high school diploma.

It felt like winning the lottery. I ran to show my mom and stepdad. They were proud. I was free. But I still had to tell my wife, but not just yet

By then, I had the diploma in the mail and was ready to apply for the police academy. She offered to fix up my résumé. We were on the phone as she typed, and I realized too late what was about to happen.

"Wait... it says you got your diploma in 2015?"

The line went quiet.

"Yeah... about that," I said, and I told her the whole story. Her reaction was more along the lines of why didn't you tell me this? I could've helped! I wouldn't have judged you! When did you even find the time to do all this as she giggled. By then, she already knew who I was, my character, my ambition, my intelligence so it didn't change how she saw me. But for me, it was a huge relief.

I'd been harboring that secret for years, lying about where I was going, all to avoid that one moment. And I learned something in it: What you do in the dark will eventually come to the light. It may take days, months, or years but it will come out.

Now, I wear my truth on my sleeve. Either you love me or you don't. I'd rather be real than be found out as a fraud.

CHAPTER 2
Don't Run from Discipline

I didn't always know what it took to be successful.

Back then, I thought it was all about hustling, stacking hours, stacking checks, working until you couldn't work anymore. And don't get me wrong, that work ethic put me in some rooms I never imagined I'd be in. But it wasn't enough to stay there. There are three things, three essentials that I ran from for years but eventually had to face head-on. Without them, I wouldn't be where I am today.

These aren't just "business" principles. They're life principles. Whether you're running a company, working a 9-to-5, or just trying to level up as a person, you need them. Those three are: discipline, presentation, and dedication.

And there's a fourth one, kind of a bonus that ties them all together, and that's being likable.

Discipline: The Main Ingredient in the Meal of Success

If success is a meal, discipline is the main ingredient. Without it, you've just got a plate of nothing. Or better yet food, with no plate.

I used to run from discipline. I didn't want to hear about schedules, rules, or structure. I liked doing things when I felt like doing them. But feelings will mislead you. They'll have you staying in bed, watching tv and scrolling on your phone instead of building your dreams. They'll have you playing video games instead of sending that email. When I look back now, some of the hardest seasons of my life were the ones that taught me discipline without me realizing it. Working for my old boss, getting paid late, never missing a day, showing up in uniform even when I was frustrated, that was discipline and dedication. I never called out. Not once in two years. And that wasn't because I loved the job. I loved the location, the people, and the conditions I was working for and it gave me accountability to show up. It was also because, deep down, I knew how I showed up in the "small" things would set the standard for the big ones later.

Discipline is saying "no" to the things you want so you can "have" the things you need.

You want to sleep in? No. You need to show up.
You want to blow that check? No. You need to reinvest either in something or yourself.
You want to react emotionally to somebody who disrespected you? No. You need to think strategically. Is this worth my energy and time?

When I started my own company, discipline became even more important. It wasn't just about me anymore it was about my employees, my clients, and my reputation. I couldn't afford to wake up one day and decide I didn't feel like being a CEO. I had to show up every single time, even when I didn't feel like it, because my consistency was somebody else's paycheck.

Here's the thing about discipline: it's not punishment. It's preparation. You're not telling yourself "no" just to be miserable; you're telling yourself "no" so you can have something better later. Every successful person I've met has that in common. They're not lucky. They're disciplined.

Presentation: How You Show Up in the World

Before you even open your mouth, people have already decided something about you. That's a presentation.

It's how you dress, how you smell, how firm your handshake is, whether you make eye contact, if you carry yourself with confidence or insecurity. It's how you walk into a room: do you look like you belong there, or do you look like you stumbled in by accident?

When I met Estie for the first time, the woman who would open doors for me in the community, I didn't have to give her a whole resume. I showed up in uniform, carried myself professionally, and spoke with confidence about my background. That presentation built instant trust. Here's what I've learned: You have to be ready for the room you want to be in, not just the one you're in now. If you want to talk to people who are ahead of you, you need to present yourself like you're already operating at that level. Presentation also isn't just about clothes and cologne. It's about energy. One of the best ways to connect with people more successful than you is to ask them questions. And not the basic "how much money do you make?" questions, real questions. "What was the hardest season of your career?" "If you had to start over today, what's the first thing you'd do?" People who have achieved a lot love to share their stories with someone who actually listens.

Once my guards' uniforms changed, it wasn't just about looking sharp, it was about the message we were sending. Clients saw we took ourselves seriously, and they took us seriously in return. That's a presentation at work.

Dedication: Doing It Great, Not Just Getting It Done

Dedication means you don't just finish a job you finish it well. It's the difference between "that'll do" and "this is my best."

When I was working for my old boss, I didn't just stand post. I built authentic relationships with clients, I solved problems before they became problems, and I made myself available at all hours. Not because I was getting paid extra (I wasn't), but because that's who I wanted to be, a person people could count on. Dedication builds trust, and trust present opportunity. When clients know you'll handle something without them having to chase you down, they give you more responsibility. That's how I ended up in situations where people were coming to me instead of my boss. My dedication and reputation was my resume.

And here's the thing you can't skip this step. Every boss starts as a pawn. You might be running your own thing now, but somewhere in life, you're still a pawn to someone else. The key is to be the kind of pawn they can't ignore. Do your part so well that it's impossible for them not to see you as a future partner, leader, or owner.

The world doesn't slow down. If you're not growing, you're falling behind. I think of life like a pool filling up with water. If you're just standing in the water eventually, you're going to be in over your head. Strong will and tunnel vision keeps you swimming forward, then provision makes you build your boat (metaphorically creating a financial cushion to where you don't have to work as hard to stay above water).

You can have discipline, presentation, and dedication but if people can't stand to be around you, none of it matters. Being likable isn't about being fake. It's about being someone people want to work with, want to talk to, and want to recommend. Your personality, your energy, your character these are all part of your brand. Let's just say it's the parsley on the meal.

I've gotten opportunities I wasn't "qualified" for on paper because someone liked me. And I've seen people lose opportunities they were qualified for because their attitude was trash.

When you're likable, people will forgive your mistakes, give you more chances, and go out of their way to help you win. That's not manipulation, it's human nature.

I like to work with what I call the "cool guy." And no, I'm not talking about the guy who had the flashiest sneakers or the highest grades in school. I'm talking about people who have that magnetic energy, the ones everyone just wants to be around. They don't have to be the smartest in the room, or the most experienced, or the most polished. But they have something that makes people say, "Man, you're so much fun to be around," or "I like your energy." That's what I mean when I say "cool guy." If you ever hear me, use that phrase, that's my way of saying, "This person has an energy that makes other people want them in the room."

Here's the thing I can teach you a job. I can teach you systems. I can teach you the technical skills you need to be successful. But I can't teach you how to be someone that people enjoy being around. That's not something you pick up in a training manual, it's something you carry with you. It's who you are. And the truth is, a lot of opportunities in life don't go to the most skilled person. They go to the person people like the most, the person others feel comfortable working with, talking to, and trusting. With the exceptions of some people born into certain positions, which isn't the case for people where I come from.

People love to say, "Oh, you were just in the right place at the right time." But I don't buy that. You can be in the right place at the right time and still miss out if your energy is off. The truth is, you end up in the right place because of who you are. People gravitate toward you because of how you show up in the world. And in business, just like in life, you don't get opportunity just because you want it, you get it because somebody gives it to you. And nine times out of ten, they give it to you because they like being around you.

Your character and your energy are a big part of this. How you show up in the world matters. People may not remember exactly what you said or what you did, but they will always remember how you made them feel. And yes, you can work on improving your presence, your attitude, and your relationships but you can't fake it forever. If you're not genuine, it will come out eventually. So being a "cool guy" isn't about acting a certain way to fit in. It's about showing up as your authentic self and letting people see the real you.

A great example of this is from an episode of The Fresh Prince of Bel-Air. Will and Carlton both interviewed for Princeton. Carlton had the grades, the résumé, the perfect answers. Will? He just had his personality, his natural, magnetic charm. And guess what? Will got the opportunity, not because he was the most qualified on paper, but because of who he was. That's what I'm talking about. Skills can be taught. Experience can be gained. But you can't teach someone to have the kind of energy that draws people in.

Now, here's the flip side. You can be the smartest, most capable person in the world, but if you come across as entitled, people won't want to deal with you. Carlton's problem in that episode wasn't that he wasn't smart, he was. His problem was he was entitled. He expected to be chosen because of his background, not because of his effort or how he treated people. Entitlement kills opportunities because it makes you unrelatable. And in life, if people can't relate to you, they're not going to go out of their way to open doors for you.

That's why being likable is just as important as being skilled. It's also why I set boundaries with people from the start. I want you to know who you're dealing with. I want you to know what's acceptable and what's not. If you cross those boundaries, you did it on purpose, and now we have a problem. I'd rather be upfront and authentic than pretend to be someone I'm not just to make a connection. Because here's the thing, what's meant for me is mine. You can't take it from me. You can't steal my blessing. And if it's not for me, I don't want it. Anything that can be taken from me was never meant for me to have.

So, if you want to understand why I've been able to build the relationships I have, why I've been able to grow my business, or why I've been trusted with certain opportunities it's not just because of my work ethic or my skills. It's because I understand the "cool guy" factor. It's because I value character and energy just as much as competence. And it's because I know that in business and in life, people will always want to work with people they like.

CHAPTER 3

Dreaming Beyond What You See

When I first left my consistent job at Cambridge Security as a sergeant to work for my boss' which was a smaller starting company, I thought I was buying into a bigger vision. He sold me the dream, talking like he was the next big thing, the next name to blow up in security. He made it sound like we'd be building something together, and I believed him. I wanted to believe him because deep down, I've always known I was meant for more than just scraping by. At that time, I was doing whatever I could to make ends meet, even selling plasma for a few weeks, which I'm still mad I did that, I was tired of it. So, when he talked about offices, contracts, and a big future, I was ready to run with it.

And at first, I did everything I could to help him grow.

I helped draft his employee handbooks and applications, showed him where to find the right links, took calls for him, handled guard interviews, and negotiated contracts. I was good at my post at the private school, and because of that, other schools started asking about bringing him on. I was literally landing him more business.

I never asked for a raise. That's not my style. But as the months went on, it started to bother me. I was running so much of his business for $14 an hour while watching him flash new jewelry and talk big. Then the pay started coming late. I'd see the client hand him a check on Thursday or Friday, and I wouldn't see my money until the next Tuesday or Wednesday. If he did pay me on Friday, it came after a day of me calling him over and over, meeting up somewhere late, hungry, bills waiting. It started to wear on me — not just the late pay, but the lack of appreciation. I never called out. Not once in two years. I worked six and seven days a week. And all I got in return was an occasional "extra" $20 in my check like that was a gift. I don't think in dollars like that. I value time and effort.

The more I watched him, the more I realized he wasn't authentic. He liked to play the role of "the boss," always making sure people knew it when they talked to us. I've never been that way. I don't need people to know I'm the CEO. I'd rather be low-key and fly under the radar. in the room without anyone even realizing I own the place. When you're secure in who you are, you don't have to announce it. But it wasn't just business it started bleeding into my personal life. At that time, my wife (then girlfriend) was working at an AT&T call center. We split bills, but because he was always paying me late, I kept coming up short on my half of the rent, utilities, even the phone bill. You keep telling a Black woman "I ain't got it" over and over, and it's going to cause problems. She'll tell you now, her delivery back then wasn't great, but at the time it was a constant source of tension.

Then I started seeing just how shaky he was behind the scenes. Sometimes he'd get payday loans just to pay me. And when my relationship with Estie, the woman who gave me my first real shot at the private school started to grow, I think he felt threatened.

Estie treated me like family, spoke highly of me, and trusted me. He couldn't control that. By then, I was building my own reputation in the community through sports and personal training. I was strong, fast, and good at boxing. visible and the work was paying off. Literally. I was making more money on my own side work than I was with him. The final straw? Every time we'd have a meeting with the guards, we'd meet at a restaurant and I was the one paying for everyone's food. Sometimes, he'd even ask me for money.

That's when it hit me:

I didn't need him.

Of course, he feels like I stabbed him in the back the moment I opened my own firm. It wasn't like that. If anything, he trained me to take his spot not because he wanted to, but because he gave me the room to see I could run things on my own. What came natural to me, didn't come natural to him. He let me see the whole game. How to deal with clients, how to manage guards, how to solve problems in real time. The difference was, I actually cared. I always answered my phone. I checked on sites. I made myself available to clients no matter what time it was 2 a.m., 3 a.m., didn't matter. People don't forget that kind of service.

Everything I hated as an employee, I made sure never to do in my own business. That became my blueprint. If you're the small business owner, your customers want to talk to you, not the middleman. If you can give them direct access, you'll never lose them. I became a Chick-fil-A in a security world. The service was different. The speed was different. And when something went wrong, I fixed it fast. Over time, Estie started noticing. She saw how I handled things and the results I was getting, and I think that made him uneasy. The last straw came when I found out he was trying to backdoor the contract. He wasn't making enough money on the current setup, so he planned to hand it off to some guy none of us knew and have me work under him without telling me.

At that point, I'd been running that site without a single check-in from him. I wasn't about to start answering to a stranger. Estie didn't like the guy either and straight-up asked why he was there. When the truth came out, I knew what it was: shady business. That's when I realized I had a choice. At the same time, I was deep in the hiring process to become a police officer $65,000 starting salary, $5,000 signing bonus. I'd already passed the interviews, background checks, and even the psychological exam. But when I broke down the numbers for Estie what she was paying him versus what I was actually getting she was shocked. She told me, "If the only way you can make more money is to get paid directly...my inside voice said start your own company." That was it. No long debate, no hesitation. If he hadn't been so shady, maybe I would've stayed. But between the late pay, the backdoor deal, and the fact that she didn't trust him, I filed for my own license. It took months with COVID slowing everything down, but once I made that decision, there was no turning back. By the time my license came in the mail, I already knew I was done with him. Getting that license wasn't just paperwork, it was a statement. It said I didn't have to depend on anybody to feed my family, but right before I officially stepped out on my own, my birthday was coming up. He'd approved those days months earlier. Then suddenly, after I told him about the license and gave him an ultimatum, he tried to take it back.

I told him straight, "Look, I'm having a baby. I need at least $19 an hour." He hit me with, "I can't do that. I don't make that much off the contract." I said, "You got other contracts. You don't have to pull it all from this one."

He still wouldn't budge. Couldn't even come up to $18. And the crazy part? I wasn't even asking to be greedy. I was already doing more than $14-an-hour work. Way more. I was the reason that contract was still alive. Whenever they needed extra coverage, I found the guards. I was the one they trusted, not him. If I left to become a cop, he was going to lose the contract anyway. And I told him that, not as a threat but as a fact. In the community, when you're trusted and liked, your clients only want you. It's a gift and a curse, you can't easily be replaced. Instead of working with me, he got spiteful. Said he "couldn't approve" my birthday anymore because of some made-up situation. Even hinted that if I went, I might not have a job when I came back. I was already making more money from my side work than I was from his company. And the school was going to work with me whether he was in the picture or not.

So, I went ahead and finished the process of insurance, paperwork, everything. The license hit my mailbox. And just like that, the contract was mine. My first official contract. That was the day I stopped thinking like an employee and started moving like a self-employed man. Notice, I didn't say the owner. In business, I think it's important to start from the employee; this helps with understanding how the working class thinks and feels. Tendencies and how they view the business looking up. It helps you gain more sympathy for your workers because you understand what they go through. Then you have to go through being self-employed. This helps with learning your own business in and out. Holding yourself to management standards, being the representative of your own brand. This helps balance out the sympathy that you would have for employees by understanding every employee is not equal. Some lack effort, some have more sense than others, respect and discipline. This is important with having boundaries and standards for your business as an owner. Now once you've mastered being an employee of your immature business it's time to create a system to turn your business into a company that basically runs itself. At that point you can call yourself an owner of a company.

The Fight for My First Home

When I first thought about buying a house, it honestly felt like a myth. Growing up, I watched how long it took my parents to finally get one, and around my neighborhood, Black families owning homes just wasn't common. It seemed out of reach for someone like me. Every time I heard about the process, the documents, the credit checks, the down payments, the closing costs it sounded like a foreign language. I didn't think I was organized enough to ever make it happen. But something shifted. Over time, I developed a discipline that changed everything. That same discipline not only made me a better worker and entrepreneur, but it also prepared me for the home-buying process. I learned that before you can run a business, you have to learn how to run yourself. For me, it started with getting organized. Keeping paperwork in order. Filing documents so I could grab them when I needed them. Running football and basketball leagues taught me that skill if I could keep schedules, rosters, and finances in order, I could do the same with tax documents and bank statements. Buying a house requires three things above all else: money, documentation and credit. Once I started making enough money to save, the possibility became real. I found myself walking through model homes and open houses, not just as a dreamer but as someone claiming a future. Being in those spaces gave me the feeling that this was possible. I told myself: *This is mine. I'm going to get it, by any means.*

By 2021–2022, the housing market was shifting fast. Prices were skyrocketing, and I knew if I didn't act soon, I'd either miss my chance or pay much more later. At twenty-seven, I had started to find my footing, testing my limits, and proving to myself that I could handle more than I thought. I didn't overthink it. I didn't even save for years in advance. I just decided: *I'm buying a house. Nothing else matters.* The process wasn't smooth. At the time, I was self-employed under a 1099 and then had to switch to W-2 status for the home-buying process. On top of that, I was paying taxes twice; I had to pay my own taxes and then pay the taxes as a business. while covering all the bills at home. My wife couldn't work because our second child had serious health issues. For the first year of her life, she was in and out of the hospital with breathing problems, needing multiple surgeries. That meant rent, hospital bills, and every household expense fell on my shoulders alone. Still, I refused to give up. I was paying nearly $2,000 in rent while saving thousands for a down payment. At one point, I had to put down $15,000, then another $43,000 for closing costs. All while raising two kids and getting taxed heavily. To make ends meet, I hustled nonstop running car washes, personal training, youth sports leagues, and working extra shifts at the school. I was working "eight days a week," barely seeing my family. For the first year of my daughter's life, I hardly knew her because I was never home. Some friends teased me, saying I wasn't being a father. But they didn't understand that the mission was bigger. I was fighting to give my kids a stable home.

At one point, it seemed like the dream was finally happening. We had a five-bedroom house under contract, and the lender even gave us a "clear to close." We broke our lease, packed up our apartment, and went to my parents' house overnight so that we were 20 minutes away from the new future and title company instead of an hour and 45 minutes, ready to sign the papers the next day. But at the last minute, the lender pulled out, saying my income wasn't consistent enough. Just like that, we were homeless, everything in a U-Haul, nowhere to go. That was one of the hardest moments of my life. But I refused to let it be the end of the story. I pushed forward, even when the first builder tried to keep my deposit. We fought through, found another property under construction, and this time I adjusted my approach. Finally, after all the twists and turns for about a month in a half we closed. The house wasn't the first one we had dreamed about, but it had things the first house didn't have, which was a huge owner suite bathroom and a huge backyard. It was a blessing. It was ours. Just down the street from my parents, with a big backyard and space for the kids to grow, I couldn't ask for more at the time.

The process almost broke me. I gained weight from the stress, lost precious time with my kids, and spent sleepless nights wondering how I would make it work. But I never accepted "no" as the answer. For me, it was a fight and I wasn't going to lose. Buying that first home wasn't just about signing papers or holding keys. It was about proving to myself, and to everyone watching, that no matter the obstacles, discipline, perseverance, and faith can turn what feels like a myth into reality.

CHAPTER 4

Moments of Truth from my real-life experiences

LESSON #1 OF 9

The World Doesn't Stop Just Because I Have Problems

I came up with a phrase that has carried me through some of the hardest seasons of my life: *The world doesn't stop just because I have problems.* It didn't matter what I was going through arguments with my girlfriend, struggles in my neighborhood, or financial pressure weighing on me. Life didn't pause for me to catch my breath. And I realized early that if I wanted to move forward, I had to keep showing up, no matter how heavy things felt. A lot of guys I knew would bring their home problems to work. They'd argue with their wives or girlfriends, then carry that anger straight into the workplace, sour faces, bad attitudes, refusing to do their jobs. But I made a decision: I wouldn't be that guy. No matter what storm was raging at home, I'd show up to work with a smile. Even if I only had seven dollars in my pocket to last me two weeks, I walked in like everything was fine. I kept a rule for myself: I don't bring home to work, and I don't bring work home. At work, I was fully present. At home, I was fully present. People naturally avoid those who constantly complain, who carry negative energy like a shadow. I refused to be that man. I never asked for handouts. I never begged. My bills were paid, groceries bought, and I carried myself with the dignity of someone finding his way.

One of the biggest tests of this mindset came when my second child, my daughter, was born. It was after I had split from an old employer and was taking things into my own hands: personal training, boxing classes, football leagues, extra shifts, whatever I could do. I was always working. During her pregnancy, my girlfriend was in multiple car accidents. At first, I thought she was just being dramatic when she complained about her stomach one night. She was up walking around the apartment crying and holding her stomach, not knowing what was going on. I was a little snappy at her because I couldn't get any sleep as this was like my only day I got to take off and sleep in over a month. She begged me to take her to the hospital and reluctantly did it thinking it would be another blank trip because she was being dramatic like she's known to do especially around me. When I'm not around or when she's around everyone else she's wonder woman, but around me she acts like a 100-year-old woman who's just helpless lol. So, when I took her to the hospital, everything shifted in an instant. Doctors said the baby was in distress and needed an emergency C-section.

I didn't even get to be in the room, it was during COVID, and restrictions kept people out. If you go in you have to stay in, I couldn't do that because I still had clients and work and bills to pay. That crushed me. My daughter came into the world weighing just two pounds, eight ounces. She was tiny, fragile, and immediately surrounded by tubes and machines. Seeing her in that incubator broke me. It triggered memories of my sister, Angel, who was born premature, just 1 pound, survived a miscarriage, and defied every doctor's prognosis that she wouldn't be able to see, walk, talk or hear and she defied all of those odds. But at that moment, all I felt was helplessness. My daughter spent her first three to four months in the hospital. And through it all, I kept working. I didn't cancel clients. I didn't back out of commitments. While others told me, "Corey, just take time off," I held to my standard: my problems weren't my clients' responsibility. Their goals still mattered, their sessions still mattered, and I showed up for them.

That's not to say it didn't hurt. Every time I stepped into that hospital and saw my little girl fighting to breathe, tubes down her throat, I could barely stay fifteen minutes before it broke me. I'd leave shattered, only to push through the next day at work like nothing was wrong. Work became my distraction, the place I had to put my pain on pause.

I learned something important in that season: being a man meant focusing on the essentials: shelter, food, security. Everything else came second. My wife handled the emotional and social side of our lives; I stayed locked on the finances. That was our balance. I wasn't always there physically, but I made sure the bills were paid, the lights stayed on, and our family had a roof and food. The night my daughter finally came home was during a hurricane. Nature itself seemed to remind me that storms will always come, but life moves forward regardless.

And that's the truth I want every man to understand: the world doesn't stop because you have problems. Death, sickness, financial struggles, broken relationships none of it pauses the demands of life. Employers may tell you they're sorry for your loss, but the next question will be, *"So are you coming to work tomorrow?"* Because work doesn't stop. Bills don't stop. The world keeps moving. So, I keep moving too.

LESSON #2:
People Don't Want What You Give 'Em, They Want What You Have

There's a phrase I learned the hard way, a truth that life kept repeating until I couldn't ignore it anymore: *people don't want what you give them, they want what you have.* At first, I didn't fully understand what that meant. Growing up, I thought if you had a little extra and you gave it away, people would be grateful. If you spotted someone a few dollars or helped them through a tight situation, it was an act of kindness. But kindness doesn't always land the way you expect it to. What starts as generosity often becomes expectation, and expectation eventually turns into entitlement. I noticed it early on, back when I wasn't doing as well, and that's putting it mildly. When I only had ten dollars to my name, the most anyone would ask me for was maybe a dollar or two. People keep their requests small if they think your pockets are small. But the moment you start making a little more say you had a hundred dollars suddenly; the asks gets bigger. "Let me hold twenty till payday." When you move up to a thousand, people want a hundred. And when you have access to five or ten thousand, you'll notice a shift. Folks won't just ask for gas money anymore; they want rent money, down payments, "investments" in dreams they'd never chase themselves.

And here's the part that stings: the more I gave, the less grateful people seemed. In fact, the very people I helped began to see me not as a friend or family member, but as a resource. A walking ATM. They didn't want the twenty dollars I gave them; they wanted the hundreds they thought I had left over. They didn't want help they wanted access. See, when people look at you, they don't just see what you've accomplished. They imagine what you must have stacked up, hidden away. They assume comfort equals abundance, and abundance equals an open hand. It doesn't matter how hard you worked for it, or what sacrifices you made to get there. They want what you have, not what you choose to give. Basically be in your position. I remember one situation clear as day. A friend came to me asking for a loan, not a small one either. He wanted thousands. I didn't say yes right away. Instead, I asked questions, the same kind of questions a bank would ask: *Why do you need it? What's your plan to pay it back? How are you managing the money you already have?* The moment those questions came out of my mouth, I could see the offense on his face. Suddenly, I was "acting brand new." I was "acting like the police or something". That's when I realized something important: in his mind I had already given it to him, it was as if asking was just a formality, that taught me people don't want accountability. They don't want to make the sacrifice and be disciplined to solve their own problems. They don't want wisdom or advice on how to build their own. They want your results without your process. They want your money without your struggle. They want your lifestyle without your sacrifice.

And here's the kicker: once you say yes one time, you've set a precedent. You've taught them that you are their safety net. You've confirmed in their mind that if all else fails, they can fall back on you. And human nature being what it is, they will keep coming back until you either cut them off or go broke trying to keep everyone afloat. The first time you say no is the real test. That's when you find out what people are really made of. Because they'll forget every "yes" you ever gave them and focus only on the one "no." Suddenly, you're stingy. Suddenly, you're selfish. Suddenly, you "changed." But the truth is, you didn't change; their expectations did. They started to believe they were entitled to what you had. Honestly, it's like ...success can alienate you from your peers, at least the ones who don't want to adapt and change with time. "It's not about where you started from, it's about where you're heading. That's why I live by this phrase. It reminds me that generosity has to be rooted in wisdom, not guilt. It reminds me that I can love people without letting them drain me. It reminds me that success comes with invisible pressures not just to keep what you've earned, but to protect it from being misused by people who only see your harvest, not your mission.

Because at the end of the day, I learned this: it's not about the money. It's about access. People don't really want the twenty dollars. They want to know they can come back tomorrow and get another twenty. And if you let them, they'll keep pulling until you've got nothing left for yourself, your family, or the future you've worked so hard to build. So again, *people don't want what you give them they want what you have.* And once you understand that, you stop feeling guilty for saying no. You stop letting people make you the villain in their story. You start protecting your peace and your resources, because you realize your first responsibility isn't to everybody else's comfort, it's to your own household.

That's not selfishness. That's survival.

This is why wealthy people move in silence. Why they don't post pictures of money, or wear too much jewelry They don't tell the world what they're making or their next move. Simply because they are past the point of trying to impress people that's mostly only listening to count their pockets. Because with every level you climb, the entitlement around you climbs with it. Which brings my point home, real money is like real masculinity, you don't have to announce it or shout it out. Masculinity like wealth shows up in how you move, it's calm, moves with purpose, speaks with precision, most of all an aura that commands any room.

LESSON #3:
Protecting your wins

Not Everything Needs an Audience.

When you move in silence, you protect your plans from outside opinions, jealousy, doubt, and unnecessary pressure. The moment you announce something too early, you invite expectations. Now people are watching — and if it falls through, you're forced to explain what happened.

Privacy protects your peace.

Nothing Is Guaranteed.

Until the contract is signed.
Until the money clears.
Until the deal is finalized.
Until the position is officially confirmed.

It's not done.

Celebrating early can make you look careless if things change. And in business, things change all the time. Markets shift. Clients back out. Approvals get denied. Timing changes. That doesn't make you a failure — but announcing it too soon can make you look unreliable.

Protect Your Reputation.

In business, your name is everything. If you repeatedly celebrate opportunities that never materialize, people may start to question your credibility — even if the situations were out of your control.

Silence builds power.
Consistency builds respect.
Results build reputation.

Celebrate After the Win Is Secured.

There's nothing wrong with celebrating — just celebrate when it's real and secure. That way:

- You're celebrating a fact, not a possibility.
- You look confident, not hopeful.
- You move like a professional, not emotionally.

Quiet wins hit differently.

Emotional Discipline = Leadership

Strong leaders understand timing. They don't speak on plans, they speak on results. They don't hype potential, they present proof.

In business especially, move like this:

- Plan in private.
- Execute in silence.
- Announce with evidence.
- Celebrate with certainty.

Because in this world, nothing is guaranteed but your discipline can be.

LESSON 4:
Embrace the chip on your shoulder

A chip on your shoulder can be fuel. It can wake you up. It can push you to outwork, outlast, and outperform. A lot of successful people started there,driven by doubt, rejection, disrespect, or being overlooked. That fire is real.

But here's the truth:

If your success is rooted only in anger or revenge, you might reach the top... and still feel empty.

The Chip Is a Tool, Not an Identity

Use the chip to build discipline.
Use it to develop resilience.
Use it to sharpen your focus.

But don't let it become who you are.

When you stay in "I'll show them" mode forever, you stay emotionally tied to the very people or situations you're trying to outgrow. That's still bondage — just in a different form.

Heal While You Build

Facing your trauma head-on is uncomfortable, but it's necessary. Otherwise, success becomes a distraction instead of transformation.

If you don't confront the pain:

- You achieve, but you don't enjoy it..
- You win, but you don't feel fulfilled.
- You earn, but you remain bitter.

Money amplifies who you already are.
If you're healed, it expands generosity.

If you're wounded, it expands ego and resentment.

Self-Drive Should Come From Vision, Not Revenge

Being self-driven without anger means:

- You wake up because you believe in your future.
- You work hard because you value growth.
- You win because you strive for excellence — not because you hate losing to someone else.

That's sustainable motivation.
Revenge burns hot but short.
Purpose burns steady and long.

Success Should Elevate You, Not Harden You

True success isn't just financial. It's emotional maturity. It's peace and perspective.

When you can look at your past and say:
"That pain built me, but it doesn't control me,"

That's power.

When you can see the positive in hard situations — lessons, strength, awareness — you stop being a victim of your story and start being the author of it.

From Spite to Significance.

A lot of people become successful out of spite. That may start the engine.

But lasting impact comes from i believe these 4 things;

- Positivity
- Belief

- Vision
- Forgiveness

If you happen to build success without healing, you risk becoming wealthy but bitter, accomplished but disconnected, powerful but purposeless.

The real evolution is this:
You don't succeed to prove them wrong.

You succeed because you believe in who you're becoming.

That's when the chip turns into clarity.
That's when ambition turns into leadership.

That's when success turns into significance.

LESSON 5:
Stop complaining... out loud

There's a thin line but a real difference between processing and complaining.

Complaining Without Action Is Passive Acceptance

If you constantly speak about a problem but take no steps to change it, you're reinforcing it. Every time you repeat it out loud, you:

- Strengthen the story.
- Normalize the limitation.
- Mentally rehearse the defeat.

At some point, complaining becomes identity.

And when you're not willing to change something, but you continue to complain about it, it is a form of acceptance, just disguised as frustration.

Words Make Things Real

There's power in spoken words. When you say something out loud repeatedly:

- Your brain registers it as truth.
- Your emotions attach to it.
- Your nervous system reacts to it.

That's why sometimes staying quiet is powerful. Silence protects your energy while you figure things out.

You choosing to go into your "metaphorical cave" head down, working the problem shows self-reliance. You vent internally, analyze, strategize, then move.

That's controlled energy.

Trauma Dumping

Venting can sometimes become trauma dumping, especially when the other person didn't consent to carry that weight.There's no solution attached or It becomes repetitive and draining.

Energy is real, and it transfers. If someone vents constantly, it can shift the emotional tone of the relationship. And sometimes people vent not to solve but to temporarily unload.

That doesn't make venting wrong. It just means it should be intentional.

Healthy venting:

- Is solution-oriented.
- Is limited.
- Happens with trusted people.
- Doesn't become a pattern of avoidance.

Is Complaining Always Defeat?

Here's the nuance.
Complaining is defeat if it replaces action.

But acknowledging frustration isn't weakness. Suppressing everything can also turn into internal pressure. The key difference is this:

- Complaining says: "This sucks and there's nothing I can do."
- Processing says: "This sucks. Now what am I going to do about it?"

One gives your power away.
The other reclaims it.

The "Cave" Strategy

Going quiet, staying in your thoughts, keeping your head down, and solving the problem alone works — especially for disciplined, self-driven personalities. It builds resilience.

Just be careful of one thing:
Isolation should be strategy, not avoidance.

If you use the "cave" to:

- Think clearly
- Regulate emotion
- Build a plan
- Execute

That's strength.

If you use it to:

- Suppress emotion
- Avoid vulnerability
- Carry everything alone forever

That can turn into silent stress.

Real power is this:

- Don't complain about what you won't change.
- Don't speak problems more than solutions.
- Don't vent just to unload — vent to improve.
- Stay quiet when necessary.
- But don't isolate yourself to the point you harden.

Discipline with emotional intelligence is key.

Complaining without action is defeat.
Processing with intention is growth.

Silence with purpose is strength.

LESSON 6:
success can breed isolation

Success does breed isolation, but not always in the way people think.

It's not that success *forces* you to be alone. It's that growth changes your environment, your habits, your conversations, and eventually your proximity to certain people.

Growth Creates Distance

When you start maximizing your potential, everything shifts:

- You seek new information.
- Your routines change.
- Your spending habits become intentional.
- Your wardrobe reflects discipline.
- Your living environment improves.
- Even what you eat becomes strategic.

Those aren't random upgrades. They're external reflections of an internal mindset shift.

And when your mindset changes, your circle naturally adjusts.

The Altitude Analogy

Climbing the mountain of success requires a different level of endurance, mentally, emotionally, financially, spiritually.

Not everyone can breathe at that altitude.

That's not an insult. It's just reality.

Some people are comfortable at sea level. Some don't want the climb. Some aren't willing to endure the thin air, the sacrifice, the delayed gratification, the loneliness, the discipline.

As you're climbing this mountain:

- You talk differently.
- You think long-term.
- You protect your time.
- You stop entertaining certain habits.

To those who stayed the same, you may become unfamiliar.

And unfamiliar sometimes feels like judgment — even if you never said a word.

The Misinterpretation

Sometimes people distance themselves because:

- They assume you think you're better.
- They feel exposed by your drive.
- Your ambition highlights their stagnation.

Your growth can unintentionally confront someone else's comfort.

And instead of rising, they retreat.

Real Relationships vs. Seasonal Ones

Real friends and solid family bonds shouldn't feel awkward just because you're leveling up. Real support adapts. Real love evolves.

But you also learn something on this road:

Not everyone was meant to go the distance with you.

Some people were:

- Childhood chapters.
- Survival companions.
- Learning lessons.
- Temporary alignment.
- Even work friends, that often get confused with real friendships.

Success doesn't always remove people, it reveals who can grow with you.

The Loneliness Is Real

Even when you understand all of this, the road can still feel lonely.

Because:

- Fewer people understand your goals.
- Fewer conversations feel aligned.
- Your problems become different.
- Your vision becomes bigger than your surroundings.

The higher you climb, the fewer people are on that path at your pace.

But loneliness on the mountain is different from loneliness in a crowd.

One is purposeful.
The other is empty.

Success Has a Formula

Success has a formula. It's not random.

It requires:

- Discipline over comfort.
- Vision over validation.
- Sacrifice over convenience.
- Long-term thinking over instant gratification.

And that formula isn't handed to you. You have to seek it out. Study it. Test it. Live it.

The Key Reminder

Don't let isolation turn into superiority.
Don't let discipline turn into coldness.

Don't let growth turn into disconnection from your humanity.

You are still you with or without money or success. This shouldn't change the core of who you are.

The goal isn't to outgrow people.

The goal is to become who you're meant to be.

And if that means walking alone for seasons, that's part of the climb.

Mountains aren't crowded at the top — not because others aren't capable, but because few are willing to endure the journey.

LESSON 7:
The Pressure of Success

Most people think money solves everything. They look at a person with a nice car, a house, or a good job and assume life must be easy. But let me tell you from experience: wealth doesn't erase problems; it creates new ones. Being broke, believe it or not your worries were simple: how do I pay this bill, how do I stretch this check, how do I put food on the table? The struggles are hard no doubt, but they were clear. There wasn't much to lose because I didn't have much. But once you start making real money, the pressure changes. Suddenly, it wasn't about survival anymore, it was about stability, and managing resources. Maintaining and growing what I had built and protecting it from slipping through my fingers. Because once you've tasted comfort, once you've given your kids a safe home and opportunities you never had, the thought of losing it all keeps you up at night. That's the hidden side of wealth nobody talks about: fear. Fear of losing it. Fear of slipping backwards. Fear of failing the people who depend on you. Poor folks often think the rich are carefree. They imagine vacations on the beach, shopping sprees, and endless freedom. What they don't see are the sleepless nights, the tough decisions, the way every new level of income comes with a new level of responsibility.

When I had nothing, I could disappear for a weekend and nobody would notice. But when you're the provider, the anchor, the one everybody counts on, you don't get that luxury. Every move you make matters. Every mistake costs more. Every risk feels heavier. I remember the first time I saved a significant amount of money. Instead of feeling relief, I felt pressure. Because now I had to figure out how to protect it. Do I invest it? Do I save it? Do I spend it on something meaningful? The money itself wasn't the blessing the discipline to manage it was. And the more I had, the more I realized how easy it could slip away. That's why I stopped believing in the fairytale that money equals freedom. The truth is, money equals management. And poor management will make a wealthy man broke faster than bad luck ever could. Another thing wealth brings is exposure. When people know you have it, they start to circle. Some come with genuine opportunities, but many come with hidden agendas. Everybody has a pitch, a need, a plan for *your* money. You can't always tell who's real and who's not, so you find yourself second-guessing people's motives. Are they here because of me, or because of what I can do for them? That uncertainty is a weight all its own.

And then there's the family pressure. Kids don't ask for wealth, but once you provide a certain lifestyle, it becomes their normal. You can't go backwards. You can't suddenly decide you're tired of working and pull the rug from under them. Once they know security, they expect it. And as a father, as a man, that expectation weighs heavy. I've seen grown men crumble under the pressure of wealth. They thought the money would make them strong, but it exposed their cracks. It gave them access to things they weren't disciplined enough to handle. It attracted people they weren't wise enough to filter. It created expectations they weren't prepared to meet. For me, I had to redefine wealth. Not just in terms of money, but in terms of peace. True wealth isn't just having a full bank account, it's being able to sleep at night knowing your bills are paid, your family is secure, and your future is protected.

And that means wealth is not freedom; it's stewardship. It's management. It's pressure. But it's also purpose. Because once you stop chasing survival, you can unplug from the matrix. And that's when the money finally makes sense, not when it buys luxury, but when it builds tomorrow. So yes, wealth comes with pressure. But pressure creates diamonds. And if you can handle the weight without breaking, what was once a burden becomes your testimony.

LESSON 8:
Manhood, Responsibility, and Self-Insurance

One lesson life drilled into me is this: as a man, you are your own insurance policy. That doesn't mean you shouldn't have life insurance, savings accounts or Roth IRA, of course you should. But deeper than that, it means your family's security can't rest on luck, chance, or somebody else's shoulders. It rests on you. On your discipline, your decisions, your ability to provide and protect no matter what life throws your way.

Too many men think being a provider is about paying bills. About throwing money around, buying jewelry, cars, or vacations to prove they're "up." But that's not provision, that's performance. Real provision is quieter. Its bills paid on time or in advance, 6 months savings for emergencies, It's food in the fridge. It's lights that stay on, most importantly, putting money away for your retirement so you don't have to work in your 60's or waiting for a small piece of social security check once a month. It's not struggling to provide the basic necessities. My peace doesn't come from flashy stuff. My peace comes from knowing my mortgage is months ahead, that my kids' future is funded, that if something happened to me tomorrow, they wouldn't be scrambling and lost. That's manhood. That's my reward. I tell young men all the time: don't depend on your woman to be your insurance. Don't put that burden on her shoulders. Her role is partnership, not protection. A wife can encourage you, support you, build with you but at the end of the day, the weight of providing safety, shelter, and security rests on you. If she steps up, that's a blessing. But it should never be your plan.

And here's the thing: responsibility isn't glamorous. It's not the kind of thing people will clap for. Nobody applauds you for keeping your rent current or for saving an extra thousand. Nobody's throwing a party because you bought life insurance or paid off debt. But those quiet decisions are the difference between chaos and stability, between your family thriving or struggling. Stop seeking applause and start seeking legacy. The flashy stuff fades. The pictures on social media get old. But the impact of discipline lasts. Years from now, my kids won't care if I ever drove the nicest car. They'll remember if I was present, if they felt secure, if I left them something to build on instead of debt to dig out of. And let me tell you, being your own insurance isn't just about money. It's about mindset. It's about preparation. It's about refusing to let life catch you slipping. Too many men wait until crisis hits to start thinking about responsibility. But by then, it's too late. You don't buy car insurance after the accident. You don't start saving for your kids' future the day they graduate. You build it ahead of time. That's why manhood requires foresight. Being your own insurance also means protecting yourself from ego. Here's the truth I wish more men understood: your life isn't just about you. Every decision you make ripples into the lives of the people who depend on you. Your kids, your spouse, even the generations that come after you all live with the weight of your choices. You can pass down struggle, or you can pass down stability. You can leave debt, or you can leave destiny.

At the end of the day, being a man means being prepared. Preparation is the highest form of discipline and love.

LESSON #9:
The Danger of Ego and the War You Could Lose

Don't let your ego bench you in the middle of the game. Ego will have you fighting the wrong battles just to feel right, burning bridges you may need to cross later, and protecting pride instead of protecting your future. Life is a war made up of many small battles — and not every battle deserves your energy. Sometimes taking the high road isn't weakness; it's strategy. You can admit you're not perfect, acknowledge your flaws, face your own internal struggles, and still stay locked in on your mission. Growth requires humility. Success demands awareness. Personal development is like climbing a mountain with a backpack, if you stuff it with pride, resentment, and the need to win every argument, you'll exhaust yourself before you reach the summit. But if you pack discipline, self-awareness, patience, and vision, you'll conserve energy for the real climb. The goal isn't to win every moment, it's to win the war over your potential. Stay focused. Stay teachable. Stay grounded. Because the person who masters their ego doesn't just chase success, they build it, step by intentional step.

Surviving COVID 19 in 2020 - 2021

In 2020, when the world shut down, my life had already started collapsing a month earlier. I had just broken up with my girlfriend and moved out a week before Valentine's Day, leaving behind the house, my son, and the family dog we had just gotten a month prior. I was sleeping on my aunt's couch when the news hit in March that everything was closing. For some reason, my mind went straight to chaos, like something out of a dystopian movie, and I pictured the streets turning into a scene from The Purge. Whether it was fear, instinct, or responsibility, I went back to the house. No matter what was going on between us, that was still my family, and if the world was going to fall apart, I wanted to be there to protect them.

Naturally, my job shut down, and life slowed to a strange silence. Days blended together, eating, watching TV, trying to act like everything was normal. We had just received our tax return, so I had a few thousand dollars in my account, but the question hung over me every night: for how long? Estie, being as thoughtful as she is, wrote me a check without me even asking. That gesture meant more than the money, it was support during a time when pride and uncertainty were fighting inside me.

Three months passed with no work, bills still coming, and my savings thinning out. I took a security job in Weston for $15 an hour, working 3 p.m. to 11 p.m., just to keep something steady coming in. A month into that job, we found out we were expecting another baby. But the same issues that had broken us the first time were still there, untouched and unresolved. Responsibility was growing, but so was tension. Eventually, I made the hard decision to leave again and move into my own one-bedroom apartment. Around that time, everyone seemed to be receiving $900 a week in unemployment and $220 a month in food assistance. I tried to get it too, but the process felt intentionally complicated, like you had to fight just to prove you were struggling. It was one of those seasons where everything felt uncertain, but every decision I made was rooted in survival, responsibility, and the quiet determination to figure it out no matter what.

Then my original job called saying they'd reopen in five weeks. Out of respect, I gave the Weston company early notice so they could replace me. Two days later,instead of letting me ride out the 5 weeks they replaced me immediately. "There's nothing we can do," they said. I had just moved in. Rent, $1,080, was due in three and a half weeks. No job. No unemployment. No food stamps. I remember the weight in my chest thinking, *What am I going to do?* I swallowed my pride and went to work for a friend who owned a thrift furniture store, driving a box truck six days a week, nine hours a day, hauling heavy furniture until I had to pack extra shirts because I'd sweat through them. On every break, I called unemployment and got nowhere, until one day I put on wireless headphones, stayed on hold for six hours, and finally got through. Ten business days for the check. Seven days for the food stamp card. Now it was a math problem: $300 a week income versus $1,080 rent. Gas. Food. Survival. I made it work. Then of course everything hit at once backpay unemployment checks stacked up, food stamps loaded with months of benefits, my first paycheck back at my original job. It felt like I hit the lottery, about $6,000 in unemployment, my regular pay, and hundreds in food support. Instead of celebrating, I strategized. I saved. Restarted sports training. Picked up side jobs. Within a month I had built it up to nearly $19,000. I prepaid a year of rent in case the world shut down again. I invested in four vending machines. I paid for every owner-operator security license and certification I needed. What started as fear and instability turned into foundation. Within three months, I went from almost unable to pay rent to self-sufficient and building assets. That pressure, that furnace of uncertainty, wasn't just survival, it was the birthplace of my own security company, forged in the fire of adversity.

CHAPTER 6
Identity Crisis

There's a real psychology behind why so many former athletes struggle after the game ends, it's called **identity foreclosure**. From a young age, you weren't just someone who *played* a sport... you *were* the sport. Your schedule, your friendships, your praise, your sense of worth, all revolved around performance. When that chapter closes, it doesn't just feel like losing a hobby. It feels like losing yourself. The locker room disappears. The structured routine fades. The scoreboard is gone. And without realizing it, you're forced to ask a terrifying question: *Who am I without this?*

That empty feeling isn't failure, it's transition.

Many athletes believe their best days are behind them because they associate their early 20s with peak physical ability, adrenaline, and applause. But that's nostalgia playing tricks on you. When you replay those years in your head, you remember your speed, your strength, your highlights. You don't remember how broke you were, how uncertain you felt, how immature you still were in many ways. Memory edits out the struggle and keeps the glory. That doesn't mean those were your best years, it means they were your most visible years.

Athletes often struggle in the workforce because sports gave you instant feedback and clear rules: work hard, perform well, win. Real life is slower. Promotions aren't based on effort alone. Progress isn't always visible. There's no crowd cheering when you pay your bills on time or invest wisely. But the resilience, pain tolerance, and competitive edge you built? That doesn't disappear. It just needs a new arena.

You are more than an athlete. You are the mindset that trained when nobody was watching. You are the dog that showed up injured. You are the leadership learned in huddles and the humility learned in losses. Sports were never your full identity, they were your training ground.

Your best years aren't behind you. Your most developed years are ahead of you. In your 30s and beyond, you have something you didn't have in your teens and 20s: perspective. Emotional control. Financial awareness. Strategic thinking. The ability to build instead of just perform.

The jersey may come off, but the warrior doesn't.

The goal now isn't to relive your athletic prime, it's to evolve it. Take that same hunger and apply it to business. To family. To leadership. To impact. The field was only the beginning. Life is the bigger league.

You were never just an athlete.

You were always becoming something greater.

CHAPTER 7
Question We All Love

Let me ask you something fun .... and don't overthink it:

If someone wired you $10,000,000 right now... what's the first thing you're doing?

Are you buying the dream house?
Calling your parents?
Booking a one-way flight somewhere tropical?
Clearing every debt with one click?

Pause for a second and really picture it. The bank notification. The silence. The "this just changed my life" feeling.

Me personally? I've always dreamed of owning a big apartment building or a hotel. Something about it just screams generational wealth. Not flashy, foundational. A property that produces income every single month. A structure that outlives me. Something I can point to and say, "That feeds my family long after I'm gone." That's not just money, that's legacy.

Now here's the deeper question:

Would you spend it... or would you structure it?

Because $10 million can disappear fast with lifestyle inflation. Or it can multiply quietly if positioned right.

Here are a few smart ways to think about it:

- Income-Producing Real Estate, Apartment buildings, small hotels, commercial spaces. Assets that pay you monthly.
- Dividend or Index Investments, Let your money work while you sleep.
- Business Acquisition, Buy a boring but profitable business with consistent cash flow.
- Multiple Streams Strategy, Allocate portions into different vehicles so no single move defines your future.
- Live Off the Interest, Not the Principal – Build a system where you spend the harvest, not the seeds.

The difference between rich and wealthy is sustainability.

Anyone can receive money.

Few know how to preserve and multiply it.

So I'll ask you again, what would you really do with $10 million?

Because your answer reveals your mindset.
Consumption or creation?
Flex or foundation?

Momentary upgrade or generational impact?

Dream big. Think smart. And remember, the goal isn't just to touch the money.

CHAPTER 8
Roller Coaster: Execution is Essential

My experience in business has been, I would say, very roller coaster-like. Imagine first getting in the seat. You buckle up, full of anxiety, fear, and excitement. You check a thousand times to make sure your harness is secure. The ride starts moving, and everything feels new. You don't know what to expect next. The roller coaster climbs higher and higher straight to the sky. Everything feels consistent, steady, and exciting. You reach a point of pure bliss, that moment where everything seems to be working perfectly. Then suddenly, without warning, it drops. Your stomach flips. You're holding on, thinking, *What the hell did I get myself into? Why did I even do this?* Right when you're about to close your eyes, the ride turns sharply. Then it goes up again, down again, twists left, jerks right, flips upside down, and shoots back up over and over until eventually, you start to get used to it. You stop being afraid.

It becomes fun.

It becomes *predictably unpredictable.*

You start to feel more in control of the ride. And honestly, it's a great feeling to see something you created through hard work start to flourish. To not have a boss. To make your own rules. To test your limits and explore the world of entrepreneurship. To be the first in your family to do something different. That part is amazing. But the flip side? That's where it gets real. Being a young CEO in the security industry is an uphill battle. Security is a field built on experience, presence, and demeanor and I have all three. But being in my early thirties, some people automatically assume I lack experience. They question whether I'm capable of running a company, or whether I've even spent enough time in the field to understand it. What life has taught me, though, is that age doesn't make you wise, *experience* does. Wisdom comes from what you've lived through and what you've learned from it. Still, I'm constantly doubted by older people who know nothing about me. To make things more complicated, i took on a partner, who happens to be Puerto Rican but passes for Caucasian often gets mistaken for the owner. Whenever we walk into meetings or meet new clients, they automatically assume I'm just a guard tagging along with him.

Maybe it's because I'm young.
Maybe it's because of how I look.

Maybe it's something much deeper.

Honestly, it's probably a combination of all three. Time after time, I've sat in some meetings, not all where clients ignored me completely. They'd turn their chairs toward him, speak only to him, and avoid even making eye contact with me. It was blatant. Now, he is great at what he does. The man could sell bug spray to a bug. So, he usually takes the lead in those conversations. I come in when it's time to talk business numbers, logistics, and strategy. But here's the part that always gets me. Once we hand over the paperwork and they see my name listed as CEO they'd say "Corey"? and I raise my hand to say, *"That's me* you can literally see jaws drop to the floor. It happens every time. And every time, I just smile and say, *"Nice to finally meet you."* But eventually, I started reading the room differently. I realized that for new clients, especially the ones who didn't already know me through referrals, it might be better if I didn't attend those negotiation meetings. That decision wasn't about hiding. It was about strategy. So, I stepped back from that part of the process. At first, it stung a little, not being in the room for my own company's negotiations. But I got over that pretty quickly, because I saw the bigger picture. I've never needed praise. I've never needed validation. What I need is *success.* What I value most is *freedom.* And that's what keeps me grounded, even when the ride gets wild.

CHAPTER 9

Importance of Having Good Credit

If you're thinking about starting a business, I would say having good credit can make things a whole lot easier. Please don't take the hard route like I always seem to do. First off, having good credit gives you easier access to funding. Lenders like banks look at your personal credit score when you don't yet have a business credit history. Strong personal credit makes it much easier to qualify for business loans, lines of credit, and credit cards with better interest rates and higher limits. Access to funding gives you flexibility. It allows you to expand, market yourself, and purchase what you need to attract bigger clients. Basically, good credit gives you a head start without having to go through the nickel-and-dime phase most people struggle through. Many suppliers and vendors will run a credit check before offering net terms, like net 30 or net 60, where you pay after receiving goods or services.

Having good credit allows you to qualify for those favorable terms, which makes managing your cash flow a whole lot easier. Strong credit helps you qualify for business credit cards and loans in your company's name. This separation builds your business credit profile, protects your personal assets, and strengthens your company's financial foundation. It's one of the smartest moves you can make early in your business journey. Potential partners, landlords, and even clients may check your creditworthiness before doing business with you. Good credit makes your business look trustworthy, reliable, and professional like you're someone they can confidently work with. Unexpected expenses always come up, equipment breaks down, clients pay late, or sudden growth opportunities appear. Having access to credit ensures that when those moments happen, you're ready. You can handle challenges without stalling your business or showing up unprepared.

That's how you protect your reputation and your brand.

Good credit gives you credibility, flexibility, and financial security. It's not just about borrowing; it's about building a reputation of responsibility that opens doors for your business to grow. When running a business, how you handle client payments is just as important as the service you provide. Maintaining professionalism in financial matters builds long-term trust and credibility. Constantly calling or pressuring clients for payments can make your business look unorganized, desperate, or untrustworthy. Clients may assume you're struggling with cash flow, which can damage your reputation and make them hesitant to continue doing business with you.

A professional company has clear invoicing policies, payment terms, and follow-up procedures. When you don't appear desperate for funds, clients see your business as financially stable and reliable. Clients want to feel respected, not harassed. A professional tone in billing ensures that even if a client is late, the relationship stays intact for future business. Structured, polite reminders such as automated invoice systems or scheduled notices are far more effective than constant personal calls. Clients are more likely to pay on time when the process feels organized, not confrontational. It's best to set clear payment terms in your contracts. Invoices due within seven days. Late fees applied after that. Send timely invoices.

Use formal reminders when necessary.

That's how you stay professional, protect relationships, and still get paid.

CHAPTER 10
Lead by Example

Leading by example sounds cliché. It's one of those phrases that feels overly simple but it's actually one of the hardest things to do as a leader. All eyes are always on you. People hold on to every word you say. Expectations are higher because of who you are and what you represent.

Leading by example is something I take pride in. I'm not perfect, but I strive daily to be better. I live by a motto I've said for quite some time: "Aim for the stars, or fall on the moon." Either way, you'll achieve greatness and maximize your potential. Being a man of your word. Following through on your promises. Taking accountability. Doing the right thing even when no one is watching. These are the marks of a true leader. Standing in front of the bullet is second nature when you lead. You have to take the good with the bad, weather storms with grace, and never compromise your morals. Honestly, it's something we can all do, but most people lack the one thing it requires: Accountability.

Giving 100% effort isn't something you should do sometimes, it's something greatness demands every time.

Creating good habits is the foundation of excellence. If you're okay with doing things halfway, not really considering the brand of your own self-worth, that lack of effort will show up everywhere: in how you dress, how you speak, how you present yourself, and, most importantly, how you finish what you start. Small habits reveal big truths. If you're inconsistent in the small things, it's only a matter of time before that inconsistency shows up in the big things too.

If you're serious about becoming better at learning, growing, and improving, you need to listen more than you talk. Period. Successful entrepreneurs and business leaders love to share knowledge and drop gems for people who are genuinely trying to level up. But too often, people with a little bit of knowledge act like they already know everything. So, when someone of higher stature or experience tries to give advice, and you dominate the conversation trying to sound like a big shot, you come across as a know-it-all without a clue. That kind of behavior doesn't just make a bad impression, it closes the door to wisdom, opportunity, and connection that could have changed your entire life. Listening isn't being less dominant. It's a strategy. The most powerful people in the room are often the quietest, because they're too busy learning from everyone else to add to their own practices.

When you're running a business that finally starts making money, you expect congratulations. What you don't expect is a wave of phone calls, texts, and emails from people you've never met before, all promising you the world. These aren't investors looking to help you grow. They're MCA guys, merchant cash advance lenders. Loan sharks dressed in suits. Fake names and fake pictures and fake stories.The moment your information gets into their system, you've essentially been marked. Maybe you applied for an SBA loan, or maybe a broker ran your credit. Somehow, your file lands in the wrong hands, and from there it spreads like wildfire. They'll call you. They'll text you. They'll email you. They might even reach out to your associates or anyone with the same last name. Their persistence is relentless because to them, you're not a person, you're a potential payday. And here's the bait: "We can get you up to a million dollars, in as little as 24 hours." That phrase *up to is* where you have to pay attention. Your eyes fix on the word "million," but what it really means is anywhere between zero and a million. Usually closer to the bottom. The companies that dangle small numbers like that often don't have deep investor backing, which means the money they do give comes with outrageous interest rates. The smaller the pool they're pulling from, the worse the terms.

They'll say anything to get you to bite. "We can offer $150,000 with two years of weekly payments." Mind you, they haven't even seen your bank statements yet. They're fishing, and the moment you reply or pick up the phone, they've got you on the hook. From then on, the numbers come from every direction, different calls, different emails, different promises. And then comes the bait-and-switch. They might even send you what looks like a contract for a $400,000 line of credit. But attached to it is a smaller, "starter" deal: $20,000 with daily payments of $400, a 45% interest rate, and the promise that once you pay this off, you'll get the line of credit with them. That big deal never comes. What you've actually signed is a trap. You've taken a bad deal that will bleed your business dry. By signing, you've sent a message to the entire network of lenders: you're willing to accept terrible terms. And once that reputation follows you, every future offer will be just as bad, if not worse.

The only escape is to pay off the loan early, rip the Band-Aid off, and take the loss. It hurts, but it's the only way forward. From there, you must grow your revenue to appeal to bigger, more legitimate investors. Otherwise, the cycle continues: $20,000 loans that only net you $17,000 after fees, which turn into $35,000 paybacks. You're losing before you've even begun. The truth is, MCA loans are like quicksand. The harder you struggle, the deeper you sink. And when other lenders show up offering "consolidation" to save you, don't believe it. That's just another trap disguised as a lifeline.

The real way to survive is discipline. Save your money. Build a cushion. Become your own insurance policy so that when payroll comes up short, you can cover your employees without scrambling. That's what running a respectable business looks like. Your people shouldn't suffer because a client didn't pay on time. Your brand shouldn't be tarnished because you were reckless with money. I learned this the hard way. I've worked for employers who paid late, or not at all, and I swore I'd never do that to my team. As a CEO, sometimes I go without, so my employees don't have to. That's the responsibility that comes with leadership.

If you absolutely must take out financing, your best option is an SBA loan. They take longer to get and require solid personal credit, but the terms are fair and the repayment stretches ten to twenty years. That's the closest thing to breathing room a new business owner can get. But if you can, avoid loans altogether. Build on your own revenue, protect your credit, and remember this: MCA loans aren't help. They're a trap, and the only way out is not to fall in at all.

CHAPTER 11

Relationships vs. business

Marriage and business are like yin and yang. Two forces that rarely flow in harmony, often clashing, yet both necessary. From a man's perspective, it comes down to what you're trying to build and how far you're willing to take your company. The truth is, the bigger your vision, the more it costs. Sometimes, it costs everything, including your marriage. Running a business is already a full-time battle just to keep up with yourself. Add a marriage on top, and suddenly you're pulled in two directions that both demand your energy. To survive, your spouse has to be stronger than you, because in many seasons they will be neglected. Their feelings won't always come first. For men, our drive comes from providing a lifestyle for our family. We gain joy from seeing them enjoy what we've built, and in our minds, that joy is supposed to be enough. But it's not always.

The business consumes you. It becomes your life, and in many ways, you become married to it. To your spouse, it can feel like infidelity. Your thoughts, your focus, your energy it's all wrapped up in the business, not them. Unless they speak up, unless they squeak like that wheel that gets the oil, you might not even notice because You're too busy putting out fires everywhere else. That's how most entrepreneurs live: crisis to crisis. You fight to extinguish one flame, only to turn and find another. And when you finally stamp them out in business, you discover your marriage has caught fire. By the time you notice, it's almost too late and you can look up and not even recognize yourself in the mirror or the distance between you, your spouse and kids.

It's not that you don't care. It's that silence looks like peace to a business owner. If your spouse doesn't voice a problem, you assume everything is fine, because you don't have the bandwidth to worry about more than what's burning in front of you. But marriage can't survive on assumptions. It requires conscious effort choosing to ask about their day, choosing to date them, choosing to invest time when you feel like you have nothing left. The truth is, the solution isn't balanced. It's character. If you have good character, much of the tension resolves itself. A spouse can forgive busyness if they still feel loved, if they still enjoy being around you, if your presence is positive when you are there. But if all they have to cling to is money, then the home becomes hollow. Money can't fill loneliness.

That's why I caution couples against going into business together. Marriage already blends lives, responsibilities, and emotions. Add money and power to the mix, and it can get toxic. Personal disagreements bleed into professional decisions. Ego sneaks in. Before long, what was once a partnership becomes a battlefield, and when the business dies, the marriage often dies with it. It's healthier when each spouse has their own lane. The husband may build his business, and the wife supports in ways unseen, offering wisdom, listening when he's on the edge, bringing calm to the storm, recharging his energy. She is the unsung hero, the cape behind the cape. The world doesn't see her fingerprints on the company's success, but they are there. And sometimes, all she needs is acknowledgement. A small spotlight. A public thank you. A moment where the business owner says, "I couldn't have done this without them." That simple act can breathe life back into someone who feels invisible seventy percent of the time. In the end, marriage and business don't easily coexist. They pull at each other like opposing forces. But with character, intentionality, and appreciation, the tension can be managed. And for those willing to fight for both, the reward is not just success in business, but the rare gift of building a life that matters together.

CHAPTER 12

Fighting Complacency and Building Discipline

Complacency is the silent killer of success. I learned that lesson the hard way. There was a season where I started counting my money more than I counted my goals. I got comfortable. Instead of chasing growth, I was consumed with what I already had, planning how to spend it, thinking about the lifestyle, enjoying the success. That's when you're in danger, because success can blind you to the truth: you're always one bad employee, one bad contract, one bad decision away from losing everything. I had to remind myself to stay hungry. There's an old saying in boxing that I live by. It's hard to wake up early and train like you're broke when you're lying in silk pajamas, sleeping in a mansion. Hunger is what got you there in the first place, but comfort is what can make you lose it.

So, I started giving myself new goals, personal and business. I always set four goals a year, breaking them into three-month windows. It keeps my head down and keeps time moving fast. By the time I look up, the year is almost over, and I've checked major milestones off my list.

One year, my goals looked like this:

- Double revenue by the end of year.
- Hire thirty more employees and expand operations.
- Save a certain amount of money.
- Publishing this book, you're reading now

Those goals kept me sharp. They forced me out of bed, even when life felt comfortable. Because here's the truth when you're driven, it's harder to do nothing than to do something. Even when the kids are tugging at your arm, even when distractions come, you push through, because your mind won't let you sit idle.

But discipline isn't just about chasing business goals. It's also about financial goals. Too many adults today live with a sense of entitlement, as if someone owes them help. They'll splurge on designer bags, concert tickets, expensive shoes, and then when the rainy day comes, they're broke and asking their family for money. That's not adulthood, that's irresponsibility. Nobody has to help you. Not your parents, not your spouse, not your friends. As an adult, you carry your own weight. And the best way to carry it is with preparation.

Let's say you make $5,000 a month. Your bills come to $3,500. That leaves you $1,500. Most people blow it. But if you're smart, you put $500 into a Roth IRA every month, treat it like a bill, and let it grow. You invest in life insurance policies that pay dividends. You build an emergency savings account, even if you're only putting away $400 at a time. You discipline yourself with cash pulling out a set amount for food, fun, or extras, and when it's gone, it's gone. This isn't about deprivation. It's about responsibility. Because when life happens and it always does you either have a cushion to fall back on, or you have regret. And regret is far more expensive than preparation. Complacency will cost you your business, your marriage, and your peace of mind. Discipline will protect all three. That's why I challenge myself every year with new goals, new milestones, new mountains to climb. Because the moment I stop climbing, I start slipping. And slipping is the beginning of losing everything I've worked so hard to build.

CHAPTER 13

Finding My Path

Finally figuring out my path came after being asked the same question over and over again:

"What do you want to do with your life?"
"What do you want to be when you grow up?"
"Where do you see yourself in thirty years?"
"What do you want to do with your life?"

It's always the question I was asked. At first, it seemed like a normal question, but over time, it became a depressing one. I was already in the workforce when it hit me this can't be all there is. I started looking around at people older than me, and I asked myself, Can I really see myself waking up at 5 o'clock in the morning doing this exact same thing for thirty-five or forty years?

The answer was always no. I couldn't picture myself doing one job for that long. It just didn't sit right with me. The thought of living the same routine day after day, year after year, until retirement felt like a slow death. So, I started trying different things, chasing money, convincing myself, Okay, maybe I'll do this, or maybe that. I told myself I wanted to be a cop, then a firefighter. But when I was honest with myself, none of it really fit. I don't even like heights. I don't like fire. And when you think about it, who actually wants to fight fire? The truth is, I didn't want to be either of those things. I just wanted to be comfortable. I wanted to make enough money to pay my bills, breathe a little, and not constantly worry about whether I could afford to live. I didn't want to live life two weeks at a time, waiting for payday after payday. That was the trap. You find yourself saying, When I get paid this Friday, I'll pay this bill. When I get paid next Friday, I'll treat myself. You reward yourself with a pair of shoes or a meal, and two years later, you realize you've worked for dozens of Fridays—but you're still in the same place. That cycle became life. And I finally said, This can't be what I was born for. It was around twenty-seven that everything clicked. I kept getting asked, "What do you really want to do?" At first, I couldn't answer. Growing up, I never had the freedom to figure that out. When you turn eighteen, your parents tell you, "You better get a job. You're grown now. Pay your own bills." You don't get asked what you want to do, you're told what you have to do. So, for years, I worked. I survived. But I wasn't living. Then one day, it hit me: there isn't a single job on this planet that I actually want to do besides playing in the NBA. And since that dream was long gone, I had to find something deeper. That's when I realized what I really wanted. Freedom. That was it. Freedom became the dream. It sounds strange to say, "I want to have freedom," but that's what I meant. I wanted to wake up when I wanted to. I wanted to decide what my day looked like. I wanted to live on my own terms without someone telling me when to clock in, what to wear, or how long I could eat lunch. I didn't want to grow old watching myself deteriorate because I'd spent decades working for someone else. I didn't want to wake up one day with bags under my eyes, my back gone out, my knees aching, and my body breaking down from labor. That's what the system does to people. It works you until you can't move anymore. Then once you're used up, you're replaced just like that. It's a brutal truth, but it's real. I didn't want that. I didn't want to die before I lived. If I die, I want to be able to say that I lived a full life, a life I chose, and that I did it my way. That realization changed everything. I stopped chasing job titles and started chasing freedom. I realized you don't have to have an answer to "What do you want to be?" because life isn't about becoming something, it's about being SOMEONE. You don't have to "be" a cop or a firefighter or a CEO. Maybe your purpose is tending to your garden, raising your family, traveling, or creating art. Maybe your purpose is creating peace. You don't have to be what society says you should be. Because titles don't define us. Jobs don't define us. They describe what we do, not who we are. And that's the freedom most people never reach the understanding that you don't have to become something to matter. We've been conditioned to think otherwise. Look at the movies we grew up watching—Bee Movie, A Bug's Life, Antz. On the surface, they're just cartoons. But if you really watch them, you'll see the message. Those characters were born into a system where their purpose was already decided. They were born to work, to serve the colony, to keep the hive alive. Sound familiar? That's us. We're born into a society that tells us what success looks like, what jobs are respectable, and what paths we should take. We're told to get in line, work until we can't, and retire just in time to die. And most people never stop to question it. When I started seeing the truth in those movies, and in real life, that's when I really found my path. Because my path wasn't about finding a career. It was about finding freedom. Freedom from the system. Freedom from expectations. Freedom from the idea that my worth had to be tied to a paycheck. So, when people ask me now what I want to do, I tell them simply, I want to be free. That's it. Freedom is the goal. Freedom is the dream. Freedom is the path. Sometimes, as you move forward, even when you're doing all the right things, believing in yourself, and putting in the work, self-doubt still finds its way in. It sneaks in quietly, making you question whether you're really capable of achieving everything you're working toward. Self-doubt is something that every human being faces. It's part of our nature. But for people who come from humble beginnings, it often runs even deeper. When you grow up seeing your parents struggle to make two or three thousand dollars a month, the idea of earning tens of thousand dollars a month sounds impossible. Those kinds of numbers don't even make sense at first. It feels unreal, like something reserved for other people. The truth is, self-doubt is not something you were born with. It's something you were conditioned to have. As children, we believe we can do anything because no one has told us otherwise. It's only as we grow that the world starts teaching us our limitations. Society tells us how far we can go, what we should expect, and who we should become. That conditioning is not accidental. It benefits the one percent. When people are filled with doubt, they settle for less. They stay employees, not because they lack potential, but because they've been convinced that it's safer that way. That's why I always say, forget about just climbing the ladder of success. Instead, focus on climbing the ladder to your full potential. Everyone isn't going to be successful in the way the world defines success because not everyone believes they can be. The ones who make it are simply the ones who refuse to stop climbing, even when fear and doubt start whispering that they can't. As you climb toward your potential, you'll encounter moments of deep uncertainty. You'll hear that voice telling you, "I'm not supposed to be here," or "What if I mess this up?" You'll start calculating everything that could go wrong, losing money, wasting time, looking foolish, and all of it will sound reasonable. But that's not you talking. That's society speaking through you. Self-doubt turns into fear, and fear eventually paralyzes you. When fear takes over, you freeze. You start telling yourself that it's safer to go back to what's familiar. Like a hurt dog running home after being struck, we often retreat to the environments that once made us feel safe. That's why so many people go back to their old jobs after trying something new. They tell themselves, "At least I know what to expect here." But that safety is an illusion. You're not staying because you're comfortable, you're staying because you're afraid. When you operate from fear, you start betting on your employer to secure your future instead of betting on yourself. It's okay to experience self-doubt. Everyone does. But don't let it control you. Don't let it make your decisions for you. The best way to overcome self-doubt is by building confidence. The best way to build confidence is through growth, learning more, gaining new skills, and exposing yourself to new experiences. The more you learn, the more you realize that you belong in every room you step into. Education and exposure eliminate intimidation. Every certification, every lesson, every piece of general knowledge you gain prepares you to walk into new spaces with your head high. Having a mentor also helps. Having someone to listen to you, talk with you, and guide you along the way makes the journey less lonely. It reminds you that you're not the only one climbing, and that even people who seem confident battle doubt too. Remember, your climb is your own. Your top might be earning sixty thousand a year after once surviving on fifteen thousand. That's still a success. The world makes it seem like you have to be a millionaire to have made it, but that's not true. If everyone was self-employed, there would be no businesses. Not everyone is meant to be a boss, and that doesn't make one person more important than another. Sometimes the only difference between a boss and a worker is that one was born into the right family or had a different skin color. So never let your position define your worth. Self-doubt is simply you getting in your own way. Once you learn how to push past it, you'll begin to see just how far you can go. When I started to really make money in my business, I didn't even realize it at first. It wasn't one huge moment. It was a gradual realization, small signs that started adding up. The first time I noticed was when a thousand dollars started to feel like ten dollars. That might sound crazy, but it's real. I remember saying, "Let's take the family to Disney. We'll do the Fast Pass, get food, and enjoy the day." Then I looked at the total and saw it was about fifteen hundred dollars. I paused for a second and then realized it didn't even sting. That was the moment I thought, Okay, I'm starting to make money now. When you can swipe your card for something you once had to save months for, that's when you realize you're in a new place. That was about four years ago, back when I started really pushing myself harder. I didn't fully go all in until 2023, but even before then, I started feeling the shift. A few months later, I saved 2 years of my salary I made from my jobs in my employee days in just two months. That was a major turning point for me. I remember thinking, Wow, that's crazy? That's when I knew I was doing something different . Soon after, I started averaging my old yearly salary monthly. Every time I thought about it, I couldn't help but reflect on where I came from, or where I would be if I never decided to bet on myself. I used to make nine hundred dollars every two weeks. That's eighteen hundred dollars a month. So, when I realized I was now making those numbers a day without clocking in to anyone's job, it hit me hard. That realization was surreal. Just five or six years earlier, I was struggling to afford gas and food.

Now, I was earning more in a day than I used to make in an entire month. I remember looking at my numbers and thinking, Am I really doing this? But the moment that truly changed everything was when I cashed a check for one hundred and twenty thousand dollars. Seeing six figures sitting in my account for the first time was an out-of-body experience. I couldn't stop looking at it. Coming from where I came from, that kind of money looked like something that only existed on TV. When you see it for yourself, it's like a drug. It lights a fire inside you. You get hooked on growth. You can never go back to who you were before. Once you've experienced that level of success, your mindset shifts permanently. You start to look at money differently. The old me, if I saw four thousand dollars in my account, I felt secure. In my new lane I would definitely panic. My bills and lifestyle alone require let's say a lot more a month just to stay afloat. And that's when I realized I had truly stepped into uncharted territory. Because when your monthly bills sound like a yearly salary, you're playing the game at a different level. And when you're here, going backward isn't an option. You can't return to the life you had before. That realization isn't just about money. It's about growth. You realize that success comes with new responsibilities, new expenses, and new pressures. The more you earn, the more you have to manage, bigger offices, more staff, insurance, equipment, benefits, vehicles, and all the things that come with expansion. To the outside world, it might look like you're making millions, but in reality, much of that goes back into keeping the business running. Still, none of that takes away from the blessing. Because when I look at where I started and where I am now, I know every sleepless night, every setback, and every moment of self-doubt was worth it. The truth is, the only way to silence self-doubt is by proving yourself wrong.

Every time you push through fear, every time you take a step forward despite uncertainty, and every time you refuse to quit, you build faith in yourself.

And that's how you find your path.

CHAPTER 14
The Only Way Out, Was Straight Through

I remember moving in with my grandfather around the end of 2016. The plan was simple: get a little privacy, save some money, and get back on my feet. At the time, I was working part-time at Walmart, hanging on by a thread. The limit for attendance occurrences was nine per year, and I was already at seven and a half, maybe eight. Working the overnight shift was draining. Not long after I moved in, I had my wisdom teeth removed. Between the painkillers and antibiotics, I couldn't make it to work. That call-out ended up being the one that cost me my job. My girlfriend had just found out she was pregnant. My world felt like it was closing in on me.

When I first moved in, the deal was that I'd pay the utilities. That sounded fair, but it didn't really help my financial situation. I still had bills and couldn't seem to save a dime. The upside was that I finally had my own room, no more sleeping on the floor, no more air mattresses or worn-out futons with springs digging into my back. I didn't have to share space with anyone. But the cons hit harder than I expected. I was isolated. Lonely. There was no cable, no internet, and no sunlight because the windows were boarded up due to home invasions in the neighborhood. On top of that, I lived with my eighty-year-old grandfather, who could and would talk for hours about anything. He didn't care if you had somewhere to be. You could try every polite tactic to end the conversation, but he'd keep going. About a week after moving in, the air conditioner broke. And that same week, I lost my job. Just like that, I went from barely holding on to completely losing my grip.

No job.
A child on the way.
Bills piling up.
A payday loan that came back to haunt me by snatching my final Walmart check.
No gas money. No food. No way to pay my car note.

The Florida heat was unbearable. The AC was gone, the windows were boarded up, and I started breaking out in heat rashes. I didn't even know what they were at first. I just knew I was miserable. The only food I had was a few cans of Spam that had been sitting in my trunk for months. Those cans became my lifeline. Between that and the occasional ten or twenty dollars from my mom or girlfriend, I'd buy a Publix chicken box and stretch it for a couple of days. But eating in that room was another nightmare. As soon as food hit the air, roaches came running from every direction. I'd eat fast and stay still, hoping they wouldn't crawl onto my plate.

That was my life: No internet. No cable. No money. No sunlight. Just hunger, heat, and darkness.

The only thing that kept me sane was my Xbox and the little bit of hotspot data I had until that ran out too. My girlfriend would come by sometimes, but even she hated being in what she called the *roach-infested hotbox.* Eventually, I hit a breaking point. I had to find something, anything. I decided to get my security license. After two long months of being jobless, I finally got a call back from Allied Barton for an unarmed security position at the convention center. It was $10 an hour, part-time, but it was a start. My supervisor was a retired military man, twenty years deep in the Department of State. He was strict. No lateness. No facial hair. No wrinkles in your uniform. Break any of those, and you got written up on the spot. That man taught me discipline, the kind that still guides me today. The first week was brutal. Fourteen-hour shifts, most of them spent standing in one spot for twelve straight hours. When I finally got my first check, $256, it didn't even matter. My bank account was overdrawn by almost $900. The moment that check hit, the bank swallowed it whole. I was still broke.

I could've closed that account and walked away, but I didn't. I knew I owed that money, and I refused to let it go to collections. I told myself, *The only way out is through.*

So, I doubled down.

With doctor visits to pay for with the expecting child, bills stacking up, and a baby on the way, I knew one job wasn't enough. I picked up a second job at the Hard Rock Casino, overnight again, of course. I worked in cash operations, counting millions of dollars every night for $11 an hour. No pockets, no freedom, and barely any sleep. But I was grateful. Between the two jobs, my schedule was insane. Security from 12 p.m. to 10 p.m., home for a nap, and then casino from 3 a.m. to 11 a.m. I was running on fumes, but I was moving forward. After a few weeks, my account finally came out of the negatives. When I say out, I mean I had $80. But that $80 felt like a million. It meant progress. It meant hope. I remember the night my check hit. I woke up at least ten times waiting for that deposit. When I finally saw the balance, $80 and change, I jumped out of bed, got in my car, and drove straight to McDonald's. That first meal, after months of Spam and cheap chicken, felt like victory. It wasn't about the food. It was about the feeling of earning it. See, when you're down bad, you learn the real value of a dollar. You stop taking small wins for granted. And you realize that discipline, even when you're broke, is what builds your comeback. Eventually, I got my car note caught up, paid back my girlfriend for the doctor visits that she paid for, and started to breathe again. The only thing I struggled with was consistently paying the household bills I agreed to when I moved in. But looking back, I realized something important. Sometimes helping family isn't really helping, it's surviving together. If someone lets you move in under the condition that you take on bills they're already struggling with, that's not a favor. That's a partnership. You're both trying to stay afloat.

So, if you ever find yourself where I was, broke, behind, and barely holding on, remember this:

- **Sleep is a luxury you can't afford.** Hustle now, rest later.
- **If one job isn't enough, get two or three.** The exhaustion won't kill you, but quitting might.
- **Don't let your accounts go into collections.** Your future self will thank you.
- **Borrow small if you have to.** A little help can carry you a long way.
- **Stay positive and keep your spirit alive.** Find joy in something, even if it's free.

Use that pain. Sit in it. Feel it. And then promise yourself that you'll never go back there again. Because when you're buried under struggle, the only way out is through.

CHAPTER 15

A Man Does What He Needs to Do, No Matter What

I have had manual labor jobs my whole life. I worked offloading 18-wheeler tractor trailers, sweating through long shifts in warehouses that felt like ovens, lifting heavy boxes for eight hours straight, all for twelve dollars an hour. Having responsibility should always be your motivation to get up, work hard, and provide for yourself and the people who depend on you. At that time, my biggest goal was to earn 60,000 dollars a year. I figured if I could make that, I would be able to pay my bills comfortably and still have enough left over to save and invest. Back then, inflation was not part of the conversation. Sixty thousand sounded like freedom. So, I started bouncing around from job to job, chasing that number. Eventually, I found a trade as a pipefitter for fire sprinklers. It was part of an apprentice program that paid 14 dollars an hour the first year, with a raise each year until year five, when I would earn my journeyman's card and make around 60,000. But there was one problem. To make it in that trade, I had to face my biggest fear: heights. I could not make this up if I tried. My next step toward becoming financially stable required me to climb 30 to 60 feet in the air every day. The irony was wild, and I also had to go to school once a week on Tuesdays as part of the program. I decided to face my fears head on because what I wanted was on the other side of discomfort.

It reminded me of animals crossing a crocodile filled river to reach new land with more food and resources. They know danger is in the water, but they move anyway because staying where they are guarantees starvation. That is exactly how I felt. Standing on a shaky scissor lift 40 feet in the air was not something I enjoyed, but I did it because I had to. I had a son to feed and bills to pay. I was tired of my account being overdrawn, tired of watching due dates pass, and tired of counting pennies just to make it through the week. When a man has to provide, nothing gets in his way, especially not something that is not real like fear. Fear is made up in your mind. Laziness is a choice. Knowledge is at our fingertips now, and the only thing that can truly stop you from bettering yourself is the choices you make and the chances you do not take. Excuses and laziness are recipes for failure. You cannot have those qualities and expect to be successful. My routine during that time was brutal. Monday through Friday, I worked from 7 a.m. to 3 p.m. as a pipefitter. Every morning, I woke up at 5 a.m. to make it to the job site on time. The sun was blazing, and the work was grueling. I was surrounded by all kinds of people, including ex-convicts, Hispanics, and whites, and I had to deal with racism and bigotry while trying to learn a trade I barely understood.

After putting in eight hours on the construction site, I went straight to my second job in security, working the guard booth from 4 p.m. to 12 a.m., Monday through Thursday and every other Sunday. On top of that, I gave plasma twice a week for three months just to earn a little extra money. After a while, my arm developed scar tissue from giving plasma so often. I looked down at it one day and thought, What am I doing?

That was my wake-up call.

I had been stuck in a cycle of overworking, burning out, and starting over for years. I realized that I needed to find a field where I could use my mind more than my body, something sustainable. That is when I decided to go back to security, but this time I was determined to take it seriously. Security had always felt boring to me before, but after working in construction under the sun, standing in a booth did not sound so bad. In fact, it felt like a vacation. I did not approach it the same way I used to. I brought with me the discipline I learned on those job sites, the toughness I developed growing up, and the street smarts I gained from surviving in hard environments. That combination turned me into a different kind of guard, one with work ethic, resilience, and composure. Before long, I landed a job as a floating sergeant covering Broward, West Palm, and Dade County. That promotion was not luck. It was the result of years of trying, learning, and doing what I had to do, even when I did not feel like it. When a man has responsibilities, there is no room for fear or excuses. A real man does what he needs to do, no matter what.

CHAPTER 16

The Land of Dreamers

Coming from where I come from,
I call it the land of dreamers.

When you grow up in a neighborhood surrounded by poverty, you find yourself constantly looking from the outside in. You see a nice car roll by and say, "I'm gonna get that one day." You pass by a big house and start imagining what it would feel like to live there. You scroll online, seeing people with things you can barely picture yourself having. It's like you're always on the outside, watching life happen for everyone else. And because you can't yet fathom having it, you stay stuck in that dreamer mindset. You hang around people who talk the same way. Everyone's talking about what they're going to do. "I'm gonna do this." "I'm gonna do that." "One day, you'll see." I spent years in that same cycle. When you have nothing, all you have is your dream. And there's nothing wrong with that. Nobody should ever be able to take your dream from you. But there comes a point when dreaming isn't enough anymore. When you're young, 18, 19, 20, 21, it's okay to dream. You're figuring out adulthood, testing life, learning yourself. But by the time you hit twenty-five, it's time to grow into your power. Society says you're a man at eighteen, but I disagree. I didn't feel like my brain, my emotions, or my creativity were fully developed until twenty-five. Between seventeen and twenty-five, I handled pressure, sure. But at twenty-five, I *became* a man. That's when I started to see things differently. Growing up, I was surrounded by people who dreamed all day. It was a fun conversation. It felt good to talk about the future. But over time, that became my biggest pet peeve—sitting around listening to people talk about what they want to do, what they wish they could do, or what they plan to do. So, I started asking one question: *What are you doing right now to make that dream happen?*

Every new year, people say, "This is my year." But if you weren't doing anything last year to prepare for this one, what makes this year different? You can't start from zero every January and expect a miracle. Dreams don't happen overnight. Big dreams can take ten years, or even your whole lifetime, to bring to life.

That's why people call it *life's work.*

Some dreams take thirty years to bloom. But we live in a generation that wants everything *right now.* I'm guilty of that too. I want what I want, and I want it fast. But real dreams require patience, consistency, and grind. There's a difference between a goal and a dream. A goal might be something you can reach in a few months or a year. A dream is something bigger than you. It stretches you, breaks you, and molds you into the person you have to become to achieve it. Most people aren't really dreaming. They're just talking. They say things like, "I could write a movie," or "I could do that too." But that's not a dream. That's just an idea that sounds cool at the moment. What bothers me most is when people disrespect the *luxury* of having a dream. Our ancestors didn't even have time to dream. Many of them worked sixteen to twenty hours a day just trying to survive. They didn't have the freedom to imagine what could be. By the time they closed their eyes, it was time to wake up and do it all again. We, on the other hand, *do* have that luxury. We can dream. We can plan. We can work jobs to fund our vision. But too often, people use their paycheck to fund distractions instead of their purpose. They'll spend a thousand dollars to take a picture with a celebrity, calling it a "memory," while refusing to invest that same money into the dream they've been talking about for years. That's the problem.

If you've been talking about the same thing year after year, but you're not taking any steps toward it, you're not dreaming, you're delusional. If you're just talking, be honest about it. Tell people, "Hey, I'm just talking," so they don't waste their time trying to help you. Because when you talk to people who are *doers*, their brains automatically go into solution mode. You tell them your idea, and they start connecting dots. "I know a guy who can help with that." "Here's who you should call." "Here's what you should do next." They do that because they see the world through a different lens. Doers think differently. If I say I want to do something, I'm going to figure out a way to make it happen. I'll hit twenty roadblocks if I have to, but I'll find a way around, though, or over them. That's the difference between talking and building. People who are just playing around with their dreams quit at the first roadblock. They tell themselves, "Well, maybe it wasn't meant to be." There's no such thing as *it wasn't meant to be* when it comes to your goals. And that brings me to something I've always believed: *Hard work beats talent when talent doesn't work hard.* Some people are just naturally gifted. They've got the voice, the charisma, the look, the body, the presence. Everything about them screams "success." But talent alone won't save you when life gets hard. When things stop going your way, when the money slows down, when the doors close, what do you do then?

That's where you separate the dreamers from the doers.

Naturally talented people often fall behind because they rely on what comes easy. They get comfortable. They don't prepare for storms. But people who work hard—they train for the storm. They plan for it. They expect it. Hard workers may not be as gifted, but they refuse to quit. That determination is something you can't buy. It's built. It's earned. It's lived. Let's put it in sports terms. Imagine two runners. One is naturally fast. The other isn't, but he trains relentlessly. He lifts weights, eats clean, gets his rest, and lives like an athlete. The naturally fast one drinks, parties, and works out only when he feels like it.

Now they meet at the championship race, let's call that race *life.* When the gun goes off, the naturally fast runner takes the lead. But he didn't train for endurance. He didn't train for pain. He didn't train for the sound of the gun or the pressure of the crowd. So halfway through, he starts to fade. The other guy, the one who trained like his life depended on it, keeps going strong. He accelerates through the finish line, wins the race, and earns the opportunity. That's life. The person who works the hardest may not start first, but they will finish strong. That's the energy I live by. Nobody will outwork me. That mindset gives you confidence that money can't buy. You start to believe that you deserve your seat at the table, not because it was handed to you, but because you earned it through sweat, tears, and relentless focus. And if I had to choose between talent and work ethic, I'd choose work ethic every time. Give me the person who's dedicated, who's learning, growing, and giving everything they've got. The one who's willing to outwork everyone in the room. Because talent fades. Looks fade. Natural ability fades. But consistency, that lasts forever.

CHAPTER 17

In life, believe nothing you hear and half of what you see.

In my thirty-plus years on this earth, I've learned, forgotten, re-learned, been mis-educated, and even taken advantage of for being green at times, you name it. And if we're honest, most of us have. What separates us isn't whether we've been deceived; it's what we choose to learn from it. I've always lived by a simple principle: Fool me once, shame on you. Fool me twice, you must really think I'm stupid. When it comes to how I view the world, I think in metaphors. It's the only way it makes sense to me. The world we live in is smoke and mirrors. What you see isn't always what is. If you can see something clearly, perhaps you were meant to see it that way. But if you learn to read between the lines, if you step back and observe the world as a whole, you begin to recognize patterns. In the simplest terms: follow the currency and follow the resources. History repeatedly shows us that most conflicts, alliances, systems, and even narratives are rooted in those two things. To explain my "smoke and mirrors" theory, imagine three people standing in a room in a triangle formation. In another room, there's an audience waiting. The three individuals begin playing a game: “Guess how many fingers I’m holding behind my back.” Two of the men stand close together. The third stands directly in front of them and must guess the number of fingers between zero and five. The guesser says, “Four fingers.” The man holding his hand behind his back secretly shows two fingers to the second man standing beside him. But when the answer is delivered, the second man tells the guesser, “It was three.” Why? Because he doesn’t feel the guesser deserves the truth. Unbeknownst to all three, there’s a camera in the room. And the camera reveals something even more interesting: the man wasn’t holding up four fingers at all. He was holding up one thumb, technically not even a finger. ***Sit with that for a moment.*** In this analogy, the three individuals represent the government, the media, and the people. The audience represents society at large. And the mystery, the manipulated answer, the partial truth, the technicality represent the simplified versions of reality we accept just so we can feel like we understand a world that is far more complex than we’re often willing to admit. Sometimes the deception isn’t just in the lie. It’s in the framing. Sometimes it’s in the definition. Smoke and mirrors. The real question becomes: who is holding the hand behind their back—and who controls the camera?

CHAPTER 18

Pizza as a Universal Analogy

Consider something as ordinary as a pizza.

At first glance, it is just comfort food, convenience, and indulgence. But look closer, and you may find that even in something so simple, the architecture of existence quietly reveals itself. A pizza is made in the shape of a circle.

The circle is one of the most ancient symbols known to humanity. It represents unity, wholeness, and eternity. In the cosmos, circles—more accurately spheres—form the shape of planets, stars, and galaxies. They move in cycles, seasons, orbits that have no clear beginning and no definitive end. The circle embodies infinity. It speaks to completion without corners, continuity without interruption. It mirrors the cosmic perfection woven into creation itself.

Yet the pizza is not delivered in a circle. It arrives in a square box.

The square represents something entirely different. Where the circle is infinite, the square is defined. It has edges, boundaries, measurable sides. It is logic. It is structure. It is containment. Squares represent humanity's attempt to bring order to what is otherwise boundless. We build square homes, design square cities, draft square pages of law—all in an effort to frame and manage the vastness of existence. In a way, the square box is our attempt to hold infinity in our hands. And then comes the final transformation.

The pizza is eaten in triangles.

The triangle is the simplest shape that creates stability, yet it also suggests direction. It points somewhere. It moves the eye forward. Across cultures and traditions, the triangle represents balance—mind, body, spirit. Past, present, future. Birth, life, death. The triangle speaks of perspective and choice. It reminds us that while life may begin as infinite potential and be shaped by structure, it is ultimately experienced through individual paths.

One slice at a time.

And so, in a single meal, the geometry of existence unfolds before us: Infinite potential, symbolized by the circle,

Contained within structure, symbolized by the square,

Experienced through perspective, symbolized by the triangle. Is this not the story of the universe itself? Born from infinite possibility. Shaped by natural laws. Lived through human perception. Perhaps the greatest mysteries are not hidden in distant galaxies or sacred texts alone. Perhaps they sit quietly in everyday moments—waiting to be noticed. Even in something as simple as a slice of pizza, profound truths whisper. Wholeness. Order. Choice.

Infinity, contained.
Perspective, tasted.

Sometimes the universe does not shout its secrets. Sometimes it serves them.

CHAPTER 19
The Meaning of Life Is to Live

The meaning of life is to live. When you break life down to its simplest form, it really boils down to two things: whether you're healthy or sick. A lot of us tie life to material things. If you've got money, jewelry, cars, vacations, then you're "living." That's what we're taught. But I think it's more about perspective. Material things are really only important to two kinds of people: people who've never had the opportunity to have them, and extremely insecure people. And honestly, psychologically, those two groups aren't that far apart. When I first started making enough money to buy the things I wanted, especially on the material side, I was excited. Super excited. Being able to walk into a store and buy what I wanted, when I wanted, felt powerful. But it got old fast.

I started realizing I was happier about being financially able to buy the things than actually owning them. You might say, "How does that make sense?"

Because once I bought it and it was in my possession... it meant nothing. I never thought I'd say that, especially coming from where I come from. But it's true. "The reward is in the journey" that phrase started making sense. Maybe it's because you're just trying to see how high you can go. I don't know. But now I understand when older people tell me, "Just keep on living." I once heard Will Smith say in an interview and I'm paraphrasing "Material things have a limit. Once you've gotten all the jewelry, cars, clothes... you realize none of it makes you happy."

Let me put it this way.

Imagine someone offers you $100 million.

But to get it, you have to lose your kids, your mother, and a leg.

Is the $100 million still worth it?

Didn't think so.

If your answer is yes, in this economy, I can't even judge you. But that's the point. Health is real wealth. We overlook it because most of us are born with it. We take it for granted. Until we don't have it anymore. Once your health is gone, money doesn't matter the same way. You might not even be around long enough to spend it. Or you're too sick to enjoy the vacations you worked so hard for. Life isn't about accumulation. It's about being well enough to experience it.

CHAPTER 20
Eviction

Man... I could never forget that day.

But if I'm being honest, that day had been coming for a long time. I was 23 years old making $11 an hour.

Rent: $1,100.
Lights: $100.
Phone bill: $85.
Brand-new car note and insurance: $475 combined.

Food. Gas. Everything else.

The math never made sense. In over a year of living there, I only made one on-time rent payment. From day one, I was drowning. Hindsight is 20/20. I knew I was at a dead end. I just didn't have the experience to pivot. I didn't know how to create a cushion. I didn't know how to save myself. Then came the 7-day notice. I ignored it. I was waiting on another check, trying to catch up on being one month, going on two months, behind. You might ask, how did I fall behind?

Car trouble. Always at the worst time.

I had a 2006 Chevy Impala that kept overheating. Finally spent $1,000 replacing the head gaskets. I figured it was worth it, I needed the car to get to work. A week and a half later, the transmission failed. Now I'm carless. Behind on rent. And just wasted $1,000.

The transmission would've cost around $2,500. That wasn't even an option. For a while, I worked two jobs without a car. One friend took me to my day job. Another took me to my overnight shift at McDonald's. My parents rotated picking me up. Sometimes I took a cab. Sometimes I walked. Eventually, I put $2,000 down on a brand-new car. Quit McDonald's. Kept my other job at Kabooms — under-the-table pay, anywhere from $400 to $1,000 a week. I figured I didn't need two jobs anymore.

New car note. Insurance. Still behind on rent. Desperate for cash, I started making side deals at Kabooms. It worked for a little while. Until I got caught. Next thing I know, I'm off the schedule. Just quit McDonald's two months prior. Now I lose this job too. Jobless. After stumbling for a month, I landed a Walmart overnight job. Three interviews. Orientation. A whole process. I didn't get my first check for almost a month. But it was too late. Four days later, I got a 3-day notice demanding $2,400. I had $1,800 ready in a money order. I called the landlord and asked if I could give her what I had and pay the rest over two weeks. Something about her response felt off. So, I held onto the money one more day. That night, I drove 20 minutes to get some oxtails from Donna's. Came back home. Put on a movie. Took one bite. Knock at the door. By the time I got up, nobody was there. I looked down. A sheriff's notice.

24 hours to vacate.

I lost my appetite instantly. At 23, what would you do? No, I didn't call my mom. Not yet. I called U-Haul. Reserved a truck and a storage unit. Called a friend to help me move. We packed everything. Bedroom set. Living room furniture, I had just bought when I thought I was "up." When I thought I was making good money from yet another dead-end job. Everything I owned went into storage. And I had to humble myself and move back in with my parents.

Every time I had to do that, a little piece of me died inside. I hate humbling myself. That's not who I think I am. I don't like living by anyone else's rules. I don't like feeling dependent. This version of Corey? I hate having to be him.

CHAPTER 21

Sometimes you learn it the "hard way"

These experiences forced me to confront something I didn't want to admit: A lot of the time, I was the common denominator. I kept finding myself in uncomfortable positions — financially, emotionally, situationally — and while I could point to circumstances, people, or bad luck, the pattern was still there. I made decisions that boxed me in. And when those decisions collapsed, I had to start over.

Starting over sounds motivational when you say it out loud.

In reality, it's exhausting. Having to move back under another man's roof — even if that man was my father — was a slap to my pride. Not just a regular slap. A face-to-face, look-yourself-in-the-mirror kind of slap. It forced me to acknowledge that I wasn't standing as independently as I claimed. Pride is a dangerous thing. When you're staying in someone else's house whether it's your parents or anybody their rules are their rules. It doesn't matter if they seem outdated, strict, or inconvenient. Nobody owes you space. Nobody owes you comfort. If you're an adult and you don't like the rules, you're free to leave. That reality humbled me more than anything else. But here's the part that cut the deepest: I realized I could become different versions of myself depending on the pressure I was under. *Desperate Corey. Hustler Corey. Defensive Corey. Prideful Corey.*

And if I didn't like who I had to become in certain seasons, then maybe the issue wasn't the season. Maybe it was the decisions that brought me there. That realization hurt.

But it also marked the beginning of growth.

And growth? Growth is rarely comfortable.

CHAPTER 22

No Pain, No Gain

That's when I started understanding what people really mean when they say, "No pain, no gain." Building a business. Building a name. Building a legacy. It's like getting braces.

Nobody gets braces because it feels good. You get them because you see the future result. But the process? It's uncomfortable. It's expensive. It forces you to adjust.

Your teeth don't shift overnight. And your vision doesn't either. There are things you can't eat. Habits you have to break. Maintenance you have to stay consistent with. Sometimes your mouth hurts so bad you question if it's even worth it. That's how discipline feels.

When you're trying to change your life, it will cost you comfort. It will cost you convenience. It will cost you the version of yourself that prefers ease over elevation.

But when the braces come off — when the results finally show — you don't dwell on the pain. You appreciate the alignment. And that's when I started noticing something else about life. Something ironic.

CHAPTER 23
Life Irony

Doing the right thing rarely gets applause. Pay your bills on time and your credit score barely moves. Miss one payment and it drops dramatically. Show up early to work every day and it's expected. Show up late consistently and you're unemployed. Ten seconds of a bad decision can cost you ten years. Thirty seconds of passion can create a lifetime of responsibility. Why is that?

Because life isn't balanced the way we want it to be.

Life is structured around consequence, not convenience.

And the older I got, the more I realized something uncomfortable: nobody is responsible for my outcomes but me. There will always be someone waiting to take your spot. To live in your apartment. To drive your car. To step into your opportunity if you drop it. Life doesn't pause because you're overwhelmed. It keeps moving. Every choice you make shapes your direction. Every reaction writes part of your story. And whether you admit it or not, those small daily decisions are building your future quietly. As adults, accountability isn't optional. At the end of the day, no one lies in that casket with you. No one sits in that jail cell with you. And that's when I realized something else: If discipline is painful, then intention is even more demanding.

CHAPTER 24

Everyone Has a Role

Running a business is also like hosting a large family dinner.

Everyone brings something to the table, but not the same thing. One brings meat. One brings sides. One brings drinks. One brings plates. But the person who sets the date, assigns the dishes, and coordinates everything? That's the organizer. The strategist. The glue. Without structure, the dinner falls apart. *Without Organization, the business falls apart.* And when people step outside their role when ego overrides order, confusion sets in. That confusion costs money. It costs relationships. It costs stability. And just like a dinner can be ruined by someone ignoring their part, a business can be disrupted by people who refuse to stay in their lane.

Which brought me back to something personal.

CHAPTER 24

Everyone Has a Role

CHAPTER 25

It's Okay Not to Fit In

For a long time, I thought fitting in meant belonging.

But most of the time, fitting in actually means shrinking.

It means adjusting your behavior, your style, your opinions, just so you don't stand out. To me, fitting in feels like being a puzzle piece in someone else's picture. You complete their design. But what about yours? I'd rather stand out and build my own frame than squeeze myself into a mold that was never meant for me. I don't feel pressure to broadcast my life for validation. I don't feel obligated to follow trends just to be accepted. Peace is more valuable than applause. And sometimes peace requires solitude. If I have to choose between blending in and becoming who I'm meant to be, I'll choose becoming. Every time.

CHAPTER 26

"Alignment Over Ego"

One of the most important skills you can develop as an adult, and especially in business, is self-awareness. Knowing yourself isn't just about confidence; it's about clarity. Knowing what you're good at. Knowing where you're weak. Understanding your triggers, what angers you, what distracts you, what drains your spirit, what throws you off your mission. When you can identify those things, you control them instead of them controlling you. Emotional discipline creates logical decision-making. And in business, logic will protect you . Self-awareness also determines who you allow around you. Energy is contagious. The people you keep close either sharpen you or slow you down. That becomes even more critical when choosing a business partner. Too many people look for someone just like them, same personality, same strengths, same approach. But real power partnerships are built on balance. You need a yin to your yang. Someone who shares your morals, your long-term vision, and your standards, but thinks completely different from you.

In business, it's powerful to have two brains on opposite ends of the spectrum. One might be visionary and aggressive; the other analytical and cautious. One sees opportunity; the other sees risk. That tension, when rooted in mutual respect, creates clarity. It forces deeper conversations. It reveals blind spots. It ensures you see the full picture before making major decisions. The goal isn't to duplicate strengths, it's to cover weaknesses. What frustrates you might come naturally to them. What overwhelms them might be your specialty. Together, you become more complete than you ever could alone.

Ironically, for a partnership to truly thrive, neither person can be solely obsessed with money. When money is the only focus, cracks form fast, ego grows, trust weakens, and shortcuts become tempting. But when the foundation is integrity, quality, service, and doing right by each other and others, the money becomes a byproduct. Sustainable success flows from alignment, discipline, and long-term thinking.

Know yourself. Choose wisely. Build with balance. Do right consistently. And let success be the natural result of who you are, not just what you chase.

CHAPTER 27

Somethings you might not know about me

One thing I've always done, with every achievement, every milestone, is measure my progress against yesterday. Last week. Last month. Last year. I use my past as a measuring stick. It's therapy for me. I actually enjoy remembering when money was tight, when opportunities were small, when the struggle felt heavy. Not because I miss it, but because it reminds me how far I've come. Gratitude hits different when you've lived without. Reflection keeps me humble. It keeps me hungry. It keeps me grounded.

Here's something else most people wouldn't expect: the world scares me.

I was raised the right way, to put good into the world, to treat people fairly, to move with integrity. But being far removed from where I started, having my own kids, working around loving families and close-knit communities, it can soften you. And in my line of work, and as a man who understands the realities of the environments I came from, you can't afford to lose your edge.

So I sharpen it.

I listen to the darkest stories. Jail interviews. Criminal psychology. I stay in boxing and fighting, not because I love violence, but because I refuse to become fragile. As crazy as it sounds, I'm naturally a good person with the ability to get bad with the bad guys. And that duality feels like a burden sometimes. But in my mind, if God has an army, someone has to be willing to fight the devil's army. You have to be able to flip the switch. Controlled aggression. Disciplined force. Protection over pride.

Another truth? I don't sleep well.

When you grow up around people who make a living off home invasions... when you've stayed in neighborhoods where doors get kicked in at 2 a.m.... When your profession exposes you to the worst-case scenarios, your nervous system doesn't just turn off. Crime doesn't sleep. Between 10 p.m. and 4 a.m., the world feels different. My biggest fear isn't confrontation, it's hesitation. It's hearing something and not responding fast enough. It's the thought of being immobilized while my family needs me. That fear keeps me alert. Sometimes too alert.

And if I'm being honest, I'm always waiting for the other shoe to drop.

Growing up, it felt like things were always eventually destined to go wrong. So even when I win, part of me braces. I don't celebrate long. I plan. I save. I invest. I create distance between me and poverty. Between me and dependency. Between me and the rat race. My peace of mind isn't luxury, it's preparation. I work extremely hard because I never want to be in a position where I can't provide, can't pivot, can't survive.

The downside? Stress. A lot of it.

Sometimes life feels like I'm in the middle of the ocean, in uncharted territory, fighting violent waves. Not always sure which way is up. Not always sure how far land is. But I have a blind faith in my ability to swim. To adapt. To endure long enough to find that private island of success and stability.

I live by a simple rule:

Either you make it happen or you make excuses, but you can't do both.

I don't make excuses.

And maybe that constant vigilance, that internal pressure, that refusal to relax fully, maybe that's the cost of being the protector, the provider, the builder. But until I build something so solid that no storm can shake it, I'll keep swimming.

CHAPTER 28
Dr frankenstein

Sometimes in life you get off to a bad start. You make a first impression that doesn't match who you really are. You say the wrong thing at the wrong time. You pass by a co-worker or that gym crush, they confidently say, "Hey, how are you doing?" and your brain freezes. You stutter. Your throat does that weird mucus thing. Or worse, they say "Good afternoon," and you respond "Good morning"... at 2 p.m. Instant regret. The kind of awkward that makes you want to punch yourself on the walk back to your car.

But here's the truth: moments don't define you but patterns do.

We've all mishandled situations. We've all been immature at times. We've all reacted instead of responded. Growth requires mistakes. The key is not pretending they didn't happen, it's learning from them. It's understanding your flaws, acknowledging your shortcomings, and applying what you once didn't know. Ignorance isn't permanent unless you choose to keep it. Reinvention is allowed. Evolution is necessary.

You are not obligated to stay the version of yourself people first met.

As you grow, your presence changes. Your tone changes. Your confidence changes. You move with more intention. You speak with more control. You respond instead of react. And with that growth comes something powerful: aura. An energy that isn't loud but felt. Not arrogant, just grounded. Not distant, just selective.

Part of that evolution is not being so easily accessible. When you make yourself available to everyone at all times, people can start to take your presence for granted. Scarcity builds value, not in a manipulative way, but in a self-respecting way. Protecting your time, your energy, your attention creates depth to your character.

And yes, some people will struggle with the new you. They'll try to relate to an outdated version. They'll expect the same reactions, the same habits, the same availability. Growth makes others uncomfortable because it forces comparison. But that's not your burden to carry.

Let them remember who you were.
Let them observe who you are becoming.

Let them adjust.

You don't have to announce your evolution. Just embody it. Move differently. Think differently. Speak differently. Eventually, they won't see the awkward moment or the old habits, they'll see the refinement.

Reinvention isn't fake. It's maturity in motion.

Make them admire the adjustment it took to become the new you

.

CLOSING WORDS

First and foremost, thank you.

Thank you for purchasing this book. Thank you for taking the time to walk through the aisles of wisdom compiled over my lifetime lessons learned through pride, pain, failure, reflection, rebuilding, and growth.

You didn't just read pages.

You traveled through experiences.

Some were uncomfortable. Some were raw. Some may have reminded you of your own journey. And if even one story, one metaphor, or one hard-earned lesson made you pause and reflect on your own life — then this book served its purpose.

I've learned things over the years that shaped me into the man i am today:

Ignorance is bliss. Knowledge is a burden.

When you don't know, life feels lighter. You move without the weight of awareness. But once you see certain truths — about yourself, about people, about the system, about life — you can't unsee them. Knowledge changes you.

It forces responsibility.
It demands accountability.
It challenges comfort.

And that burden? It's not meant to break you. It's meant to build you.

Another truth I've come to live by:

Welcome failure. Embrace embarrassment.

Failure is not the enemy.
Embarrassment is not the end.

Negativity is everywhere — in rooms, online, in conversations, in doubt, sometimes even in your own head. But if there is no positivity around you, learn how to use negativity as fuel. Let doubt sharpen you. Let criticism discipline you. Let rejection redirect you. If people talk about you — good. If they underestimate you — better.

If they count you out — perfect.

That's fuel.

Growth doesn't require applause. It requires endurance. Before I close, I'll leave you with something simple. A riddle:

Everyone has me.
Some more, some less.
Some run out.
You can trade me.
But if you waste me,
You can never get me back.

What am I? **Time.**

Time is the only currency you can't replenish. You can lose money and make it back. You can lose status and rebuild it.

You can lose possessions and replace them. But once time is gone, it's gone. So, use it wisely. Spend it intentionally.

Invest it where it multiplies. Protect it from those who waste it. And most importantly, live. Because at the end of it all, the meaning of life really is simple. To live. Not just exist. Not just accumulate. Not just survive. But live with awareness. Live with intention. Live with discipline. Live with purpose.

If this book did anything for you, I hope it reminded you of that. Now close these pages and go make your time count.

ABOUT THE AUTHOR

Corey Antonio Cowart Jr. was born in Hollywood, Florida, and raised in Fort Lauderdale, where he learned early on that life's greatest lessons aren't always taught in classrooms. A self-proclaimed *"systematically uneducated"* man, Corey credits the world and experience as his greatest teachers.

Like many young dreamers, his childhood aspirations were shaped by what he saw: he wanted to be an athlete, an entertainer, a star. But as he grew, so did his understanding of freedom, not just the kind that comes with success, but the kind that comes from self-sufficiency. Today, Corey is a businessman and founder of CAC Security, a company he built from the ground up, scaling it from a one-man operation to a seven-figure enterprise through resilience, discipline, and faith in his own potential.

As the second oldest of six siblings and a father of three, Corey has made it his mission to model manhood rooted in accountability, problem-solving, and legacy-building. His book serves as a message to his sons, his grandsons, and to men everywhere who feel unseen, underestimated, or limited by their circumstances. He believes that success isn't about being rich, it's about maximizing your potential, owning your work, and standing firm in your worth. As he often says, *"Find something you're good at and become great at it. Be known for your greatness, not your busyness."*

Through his writing and his work, Corey aims to reach those who were never given a fair shot; the ones still learning to unlearn, still fighting to find themselves, and still daring to dream beyond what they've been exposed to. His story is proof that even without a roadmap, you can still reach the top - one step, one lesson, and one choice at a time.

www.ingramcontent.com/pod-product-compliance
Lightning Source LLC
LaVergne TN
LVHW010839120826

845149LV00017B/3316
* 9 7 9 8 9 9 5 1 7 2 2 2 2 *